Plato

Selections from Plato, the Philosophy of Socrates

The Apology, the Phædo

Plato

Selections from Plato, the Philosophy of Socrates
The Apology, the Phædo

ISBN/EAN: 9783337022129

Printed in Europe, USA, Canada, Australia, Japan

Cover: Foto ©Thomas Meinert / pixelio.de

More available books at **www.hansebooks.com**

SELECTIONS FROM PLATO

THE PHILOSOPHY OF SOCRATES

THE APOLOGY   THE PHÆDO

From the Translation by Taylor, with Introduction and
Notes by

HARRY T. NIGHTINGALE

Instructor in History and English, South Division High School
Chicago

CHICAGO
AINSWORTH & COMPANY
1897

INTRODUCTION TO THE APOLOGY.

THE fifth century before Christ was the first truly glorious period of Grecian History. It was a glorious period for the world, and glorious for the world because glorious for Greece. The despots of Persia—that ancient abode of extreme, sickening conservatism—had made great but futile efforts to strangle the new and vigorous young child of liberty. To the Asiatic East, Greece was an ill-shapen child, and, according to custom, as much Grecian as barbarian, the Persian felt she should be destroyed. He would not run the risk of allowing her merely to be exposed to death on some Mt. Ida of commercial and military isolation; he would be positive. Greece exposed, alone, free, would surely flourish. She must be murdered directly.

We all know the stories of Marathon and Thermopylæ, of Salamis and Platæa. We know how those freeborn men of Greece refused to bow to the overlordship of their eastern enemies, refused adoption at the hands of Persia, refused the enervating life and certain death that was planned for them. When, about 460 B. C., Greece had safely emerged from the conflict with despotism and was well embarked on her great career of literary, philosophical and political activity, the renowned city of Athens, the πόλις Ἀθῆναι that Xerxes had once burned, was rapidly becoming the greatest city in the world. Its streets were filled with men of thought and action. Its academies, its schools, its public meetings, its conclaves, its banquets—in short, its public and private, political, literary and social gatherings were all attended by the most energetic men of the then world. Minds quickened by the free thought of pastoral Greece, bodies strengthened and invigorated by the free atmosphere of Grecian liberty, came together for mutual benefit and general progress. There were statesmen like Pericles, who formed and executed great policies of public weal; writers of tragedy like Sophocles, who laid the foundation of the modern drama; comic poets, like Aristophanes, who ridiculed the public men of the time; sculptors, like Phidias, whose works no chisel has ever dared to excel; philosophers, like Anaxagoras, who was pointing to a supreme intelligence as the author of all nature.

Chief among the latter, as judged by succeeding ages, and by our own time, was Socrates. Toward the latter part of the fifth century, B. C., he was well advanced in years, with an accumulated knowledge and wisdom which comes to fertile and expanding minds. He went about the city talking with all men on all interesting subjects of reflection, asking questions of all who would answer, inciting men to think, that they might with their own wisdom see the truth. He seemed to speak of strange things and utter strange words. He did not appear to con-

INTRODUCTION TO THE APOLOGY.

form entirely to the established lines of thought. There were men who made a business of teaching wisdom. Socrates cast a doubt about the certainty of all their doctrines. He said "Is that surely so? Can there be no advance, no deviation whatever?" These were the Sophists. That they might lessen Socrates' influence with the people and thereby increase their own, they charged him with corrupting the youth, with teaching strange thoughts, and strange gods. They said "Socrates does not worship the city's gods; he confounds men's minds." The great poet Aristophanes, in his comedy, "The Clouds," was, in a measure, the mouthpiece of a certain public opinion when he ridiculed the great thinker with being a strange and harmful reformer. Men of Athens laughed; some scorned or tried to scorn the fearless questioner. He loved truth. They mocked him. He was brave and gentle. They jeered, they goaded him. He was calm and thoughtful. He was confident in his own position, for he felt that he was eloquent who speaks the truth.[1]

Masses of men must rely on the superior work of men more generously endowed with power of mind and body. Men great in action and in thought must do and perform work for thousands. Such are the leaders of great reforms, men who have made epochs of history. One such man comprises within himself many men. One has complete within himself the genius, faculties and resources of many.

[1] How does this statement conform with the modern idea of eloquence?

In the first part of the Apology, Socrates speaks of the accusation against him as follows: "It is this: Socrates acts wickedly, and with criminal curiosity investigates things under the earth and in the heavens. He also makes the worse appear the better argument; and he teaches these things to others." Such an accusation might be brought against every reformer this world has known. For in the opinion of most contemporaries reformers act wickedly. They are wicked because they are "curious" to learn more than they already know.

Socrates pretended to no wisdom; which very fact showed he possessed it. The wise man is modest, and of all wise men, the inquiring Socrates was the most modest. Yet he thought it was "a beautiful thing if one man could instruct others." He was charged with pretending to supernatural wisdom. He denied it and said only that he did have some human. But even that wisdom to which he did modestly lay claim was the wisdom of the man who knows that he knows nothing. To an inquiry as to who was the wisest of men, the Oracle of Delphi answered that Socrates was. This incensed the professional wise men of Athens. Socrates did not profess at first to know why he should be called the wisest of men. So in his customary way he inquires; he asks questions; he goes among the politicians and talks with them. A certain politician pretends to know everything. Therefore Socrates feels sure the politician is not wiser than he, and the Oracle so far is correct. He goes among the poets. They are the same as the politicians. Then he seeks the company of the artificers. He finds they do know something and have some wisdom, but the Oracle's dictum is still true. For the artificers pretend to know many other things, which they do not at all, and Socrates pretends to know nothing.

The charges against him were general. No direct charge could be found. They were such as might be made against any man of active speculative thought. Men hated him because of the very wisdom of his modesty. With his very simplicity of thought and action he confounded his accusers. They contradicted themselves. He puzzled the Athenians as all reformers puzzle their contemporaries. He puzzled them not so much by his positive opinion as by their ignorance, and superstitious fear of any intimation of any change of thought. Like all men who think fearlessly, freely and independently, he was accused of ungodliness and heresy.

Socrates was tried before the dicasts, the great court of justice in Athens, on the charge of corrupting the minds of men, and not worshiping the city's gods. He made his defense in person, and in the "Apology of Socrates," which follows, we have Plato's version of Socrates' speech. We have no means of being sure just how much of what Plato gives us Socrates actually said. In the Memorabilia of Zenophon, the Greek soldier and leader of the Retreat of the Ten Thousand, the account of Socrates' defense agrees substantially with Plato's; nevertheless the Apology of Socrates is a work of Plato. Socrates left no writings. He simply conversed, talked, discussed. He went about the streets doing good. He was a man of his own age talking to men of his own time. It was left for his great disciple, Plato, in some respects a greater thinker than Socrates, to give to all the world the words and sayings of the master. In giving those words, Plato has added many of his own. He has interspersed the sentences of Socrates with those of Plato. Strictly, therefore, we must call this defense, "Plato's Apology of Socrates."

The two philosophers should always be considered together; Socrates, the master; Plato, a number of years younger, the disciple; bound together by ties of love and mutual respect. We must note the deep moral tone that pervades the purposes of both men. We see how unconcerned Socrates is about death, looking upon death as only a step to a new life. It is this wonderful happy contentment with all the vicissitudes of life and death that gives Socrates' speech the easy flowing style it has. It is a philosophical resignation that quiets him and prepares him for the fatal hemlock. These moments of passive satisfaction may impress the reader with a feeling that Socrates was egotistic, that he was egostistically self-satisfied. In such periods of his speech he glows with irony, superiority, audacity. Yet these moments which may appear the weakest, are really the strongest. They show us the great man, confident of his own integrity and the righteousness of his purpose, yielding to the feeling and despotic power of the people, people who could not or would not understand him.

The true impression of Socrates making his defense before the dicasts has been well put by Cicero. This great orator and literary critic speaks of him as appearing before his judges as a master, not as a suppliant, being tried. And as a master of thought we must conceive him, yet as a master as gentle as a suppliant but as fearless and unabashed as a king. He cared not for men. He was no respecter of persons. He treated all men alike.

ARGUMENT OF THE APOLOGY.

THE apology of Socrates before the judges is divided into three parts: the defense; the speech concerning the mitigation of the penalty; his last words to the Athenians. The speech begins with a denunciation of studied rhetoric. Socrates seeks only the truth and will not clothe his arguments with the studied phrases of professional rhetoricians. He wishes to speak in his customary way. He begs their indulgence that he may use his own ordinary and homely phrases in which to defend himself against his accusers.

He has been accused of many things, but the chief accusation is comprised in the charge that he teaches strange gods. There are two kinds of accusers who appear against him.[1] (1) The comic poets charge that he is a student of physics, that he is "studious of things on high and exploring everything under the earth." Socrates admits a love for knowledge and for such investigation, but he disclaims any acquaintance with the science. He says that there are men who can and do teach something in this branch, but that he can not and never has taught anything in that line. But why should men be condemned for teaching physics? (In Socrates' time it was considered wicked to be too wise and "curious" about physical phenomena. Such things were left to the gods.) (2) Many men charged him with teaching for pay. He denies it. Yet he has heard of good men who teach for money and envies them their ability. A man should be paid for teaching and caring for a young man, as well as a groom for keeping a colt in trim. So Socrates, though he tells the Athenians there is no wrong in receiving pay for teaching, is yet innocent of the charge which some would use

[1] See the clouds of Aristophanes. Ver. 112 et seq et ver. 188.

against him. He then tells the story of the Delphic oracle; how Chærepho had inquired of the priestess if there were any more wise than Socrates, and her reply that there were none. He tells of his endeavors to understand the truth of the Delphic answer; how he went among the politicians, the poets, the craftsmen; how he learned of their conceit and finally understood the oracle. He knew that he knew nothing. Such a confession made enemies of the professors of knowledge; for Socrates would spoil their trade. The wisest is he who knows that his wisdom is nothing. Divinity is truly wise; wise in reality. Socrates wishes to impress upon men the nothingness of human when compared with divine knowledge.

Melitus is the chief accuser and he says that Socrates is heretical and believes that the moon is earth. Socrates shows that this doctrine of the moon and sun comes from Anaxagoras, the philosopher, and that it is disseminated in the theatre and that it would thus be foolish for him to pretend to originate a doctrine which comes from other sources.

In several pages following Socrates completely confounds his accusers concerning their charges of religious heresy. The vulgar will accuse him of bringing death upon himself by teaching new doctrines. Yet no man should fear death. "For no one knows but that death may be to man the greatest of goods." He obeys God rather than man. He considers only "whether he acts justly, or unjustly, like a good or a bad man." He cares not for temporary things, but for eternal. He "loves and honors Athenians, but obeys divinity rather than them." He does not defend himself for fear of death, but for the principle of truth for which he pleads.

Socrates explains his wishes and desires in talking with and questioning men. He does not desire to be the preceptor of any one. Yet if any wish to talk and communicate with him he will not and has not repulsed them. He wishes no reward but the mutual good both he and his companions may gain. He offers himself to be questioned by the rich and poor, and if any one will answer his questions, he in turn will tell all he can in reply to others.

Many men before him have been tried before the dicasts and many have resorted to methods of touching the sentiments of pity, in order to play upon the weakness of their judges. But, though in the face of death he will not indulge in such practices; yet he has relatives, and friends through pity for whom, he might excite the judges' leniency. "He is not sprung from an oak nor from a rock, BUT FROM MEN;" yet he is willing to die; he will suffer nothing dreadful by dying. He would not have earthly immortality, even if they did not put him to death. Death is immortality to him, however it comes.

The first part of the apology, the defense proper, closes with a strenuous and beautiful assertion of his belief in the gods, and a reference to Athenians and "to divinity to judge concerning me such things as will be best both for me and you."

At this point the vote was taken and Socrates was condemned by a small majority of the judges.

According to the custom of the law the prisoner was allowed to choose one of three punishments; namely, perpetual imprisonment, a fine, or banishment. Socrates avails himself of the opportunity, but very unexpectedly to the judges, he tells them that he thinks he ought to be maintained at public expense in the Prytaneum which was the Olympic victor's reward. He has given up riches and power for the sake of philosophy. He is poor because he has spent his time in benefiting Athens and Athenians. He can not choose to pay a fine, for he has no money. He can not choose exile, for foreigners would not listen to him, if his own countrymen will not; and he would not care to live if he could not continue his investigations of truth. But Socrates' friends, Plato and others, persuade him to accept a fine and they act as his securities. But Socrates had incensed the judges by what they considered insolence when he said he thought he deserved a reward rather than punishment. They condemned him to die.

Socrates closes with a powerful rebuke of the Athenians. He tells them that which literally proves true, that they will meet with a fearful retribution. He prophecies that those who condemn him will suffer, for men will see the light and will say that Socrates was wrongfully murdered. Many whom he has restrained will grow more enthusiastic in his favor and more bitter against his enemies. His disciples will continue his work. Those who have wronged him will suffer for their unrighteousness.

Very appropriately the final words of the apology are on the subject of death. That great mystery was the favorite theme of all his discourses, and now that he was about to meet it himself he seemed more happy in its discussion than ever before. Death is not an evil, said Socrates. It is a positive good or nothing. It is a long dreamless sleep or a migration to another place. Either was a happy lot. If the latter, what joy would he experience in the company of those who had gone before, with Homer's heroes and other Greeks! Nothing is evil to a good man. He is willing to die. It will be better for him. He exhorts all men to pay more attention to virtue than to anything else. With these words of kindness and love he gives himself over to die with an equanimity and self-resignation characteristic only of a great soul.

THE APOLOGY OF SOCRATES.

Pace through thy cell, old Socrates, cheerily to and fro;
  Keep to the purpose of thy soul, and let the poison flow.
They may crush to earth the lamp of clay that holds a light divine,
  But they cannot quench the power of thought by all their deadly wine.

They cannot blot thy spoken words from the memory of man
  By all the poison ever was brewed since time its course began;
For still the world goes round and round, and the genial seasons run
  And ever the right comes uppermost, and ever is justice done.

Spoken on his Trial before the Court of the Heliæa.

I KNOW not, O Athenians, how you may have been affected by my accusers: I indeed have through them almost forgotten myself, so persuasively have they spoken; though, as I may say, they have not asserted anything which is true. But among the multitude of their false assertions I am most surprised at this, in which they say that you ought to beware of being deceived by me, as if I were an eloquent speaker. For that they should not be ashamed of asserting that which facts will immediately confute, since in the present instance I shall appear to you to be by no means eloquent,—this seems to me to be the consummation of impudence; unless they call him eloquent who speaks the truth. For, if they assert this, I shall indeed acknowledge myself to be a rhetorician[1], though not according to their conceptions. They have not then as I said, asserted anything which is true;

---

[1] Socrates refers to the professional rhetoricians, who persecute him, but who really should be tried rather than he.

but from me you will hear all the truth. Not, by Zeus, O Athenians, that you will hear from me a discourse splendidly decorated with words and phrases, and adorned in other respects like the harangues of these men; but you will hear me speaking in such language as may casually present itself. For I am confident that what I say will be just, nor let anyone of you expect it will be otherwise: for it does not become one of my age to come before you like a lad with a studied discourse. And, indeed, I very much request and beseech you, O Athenians, that if you should hear me apologizing in the same terms and modes of expression which I am accustomed to use in the Forum, on the Exchange and Public Banks, and in other places, where many of you have heard me, —that you will neither wonder nor be disturbed on this account, for the case is as follows: — I now for the first time come before this tribunal, though I am more than seventy years old; and consequently I am a stranger to the mode of speaking which is here adopted. As, therefore, if I were in reality a foreigner, you would pardon me for using the language and the manner in which I had been educated, so now I request you, and this justly, as it appears to me, to suffer the mode of my diction, whether it be better or worse; and to attend to this, whether I speak what is just or not: for this is the virtue of a judge, as that of an orator is to speak the truth.

In the first place, therefore, O Athenians, it is just that I should answer the first false accusations of me, and my first accusers, and afterwards the latter accusations, and the latter accusers. For many have been accusers of me to you for many years, and who have asserted nothing true, of whom I am more afraid than of

Anytus and his accomplices, though these indeed are powerful in persuading; but those are still more so, who, having been conversant with many of you from infancy, have persuaded you and accused me falsely. For they have said, that there is one Socrates, a wise man, studious of things on high, and exploring everything under the earth, and who also can make the worse appear the better argument. These men, O Athenians, who spread this report are my dire accusers. For those who hear it think that such as investigate these things do not believe that there are gods. In the next place, these accusers are numerous, and have accused me for a long time. They also said these things to you in that age in which you would most readily believe them, some of you being boys and lads; and they accused me unchallenged, there being no one to speak in my defense. But that which is most irrational of all is this, that neither is it possible to know and tell their names, except some one of them should be a comic poet. Such however as have persuaded you by employing envy and calumny, together with those who, being persuaded themselves, have persuaded others,— with respect to all these, the method to be adopted is most dubious. For it is not possible to call them to account here before you, nor to confute any one of them; but it is necessary, as if fighting with shadows, to make my defense and refutation without any to answer me. Consider, therefore, as I have said that my accusers are twofold, some having accused me lately, and others formerly; and think that it is necessary I should answer the latter of these first; for you also have heard these my accusers, and much more than you have those by whom I have been recently accused. Be it so. I must defend myself then, O Athenians, and endeavor in this so short a space of time to remove from you the calumny which you have so long entertained. I wish, therefore, that this my defense may effect something better both for you and me, and that it may contribute to some more important end. I think, however, that it will be attended with difficulty, and I am not entirely ignorant what the difficulty is. At the same time let this terminate as Divinity pleases. It is my business to obey the law, and to make my apology.

3. Let us repeat, therefore, from the beginning what the accusation was, the source of that calumny in which Melitus confiding brought this charge against me. Be it so. What then do my accusers say? For their accusation must be formally recited as if given upon oath. It is this: SOCRATES ACTS WICKEDLY, AND WITH CRIMINAL CURIOSITY INVESTIGATES THINGS UNDER THE EARTH, AND IN THE HEAVENS. HE ALSO MAKES THE WORSE TO APPEAR THE BETTER ARGUMENT; AND HE TEACHES THESE THINGS TO OTHERS. Such is the accusation: for things of this kind you also have yourselves seen in the comedy of Aristophanes; for there one Socrates is exhibited, who affirms that he walks upon the air, and idly asserts many other trifles of this nature; of which things, however, I neither know much nor little. Nor do I say this as despising such a science, if there be any one wise about things of this kind, lest Melitus should charge me with this as a new crime, but because, O Athenians, I have no such knowledge. I adduce many of you as witnesses of this, and I call upon such of you as have at any time heard me discoursing, and there are many such among you, to teach and declare to each other if you have ever heard me speak much or little about things of

this kind. And from this you may know that other things also, which the multitude assert of me, are all of them of a similar nature; for no one of them is true. For neither if you have heard any one assert that I attempt to teach men, and that I make money by so doing,—neither is this true. This, indeed, appears to me to be a beautiful thing, if some one is able to instruct men, like Gorgias the Leontine, Prodicus the Cean, and Hippias the Elean.[1] For each of these, in the several cities which he visits, has the power of persuading the young men, who are permitted to apply themselves to such of their own countrymen as they please without any charge, to adhere to them only, and to give them money and thanks besides for their instruction. There is also another wise man, a Parian, who I hear has arrived hither. For it happened that I once met with a man who spends more money on the sophists than all others,—I mean Callias the son of Hipponicus. I therefore asked him, for he has two sons, O Callias, said I, if your two sons were two colts or calves, should we not have some one to take care of them, who would be paid for so doing, and who would make them beautiful, and the possessors of such good qualities as belong to their nature? But now, since your sons are men, what master do you intend to have for them? Who is there that is scientifically knowing in human and political virtue of this kind? For I think that you have considered this, since you have sons. Is there such a one, said I, or not? There certainly is, he replied. Who is he? said I. And whence is he? And for how much money does he teach? It is Evenus the Parian, said he, Socrates, and he teaches for five

[1] No attempt should be made to remember the men mentioned in either the Apology or the Phædo, as they are not of sufficient historical importance.

minæ [$75.00]. And I indeed considered Evenus to be a happy and fortunate man, if he in reality possesses this art, and so elegantly teaches. I therefore should also glory and think highly of myself, if I had a scientific knowledge of these things; but this, O Athenians, is certainly not the case.

Perhaps, however, some one may reply: But, Socrates, what have you done then? Whence have these calumnies against you arisen? For unless you had more curiously employed yourself than others, and had done something different from the multitude, so great a rumor would never have been raised against you. Tell us, therefore, what it is, that we may not pass an unadvised sentence against you. He who says these things appears to me to speak justly, and I will endeavor to show you what that is which has occasioned me this appellation and calumny. Hear, therefore; and though perhaps I shall appear to some of you to jest, yet be well assured that I shall tell you all the truth. For I, O Athenians, have acquired this name through nothing else than a certain wisdom. But of what kind is this wisdom? Perhaps it is human wisdom. For this in reality I appear to possess. Those, indeed, whom I just now mentioned possessed perhaps more than human wisdom, which I know not how to denominate, for I have no knowledge of it. And whoever says that I have, speaks falsely, and asserts this to calumniate me. But, O Athenians, be not disturbed if I appear to speak somewhat magnificently of myself. For this which I say is not my own assertion, but I shall refer it to one who is considered by you as worthy of belief. For I shall adduce to you the Delphic Deity himself as a testimony of my wisdom, if I have any, and of the quality it possesses. You certainly then know Chærepho; he was my associate from a youth, was familiar with most of you, and accompanied you in and returned with you from your exile. You know, therefore, what kind of a man Chærepho was, and how eager in all his undertakings. He then, coming to Delphi, had the boldness to consult the oracle about this particular. Be not, as I said, O Athenians, disturbed, for he asked if there was any one more wise than I am. And the Pythian priestess answered that there was not any one more wise. His brother can testify to you the truth of these things, for Chærepho himself is dead.

Consider then on what account I assert these things, for I am going to inform you whence this calumny against me arose. When I heard this answer of the oracle, I thus considered with myself, What does the God say? and what does he obscurely signify? For I am not conscious to myself that I am wise, either in a great or in a small degree. What then does he mean in saying that I am most wise? For he does not lie, since that is not possible to him. And for a long time, indeed, I was dubious what he could mean. Afterward with considerable difficulty, I betook myself to the following mode of investigating his meaning. I went to one of those who appear to be wise men, that here if anywhere I might confute the prediction, and evince to the oracle that this man was more wise than I. Surveying, therefore, this man (for there is no occasion to mention his name, but he was a politician); while I beheld him and discoursed with him, it so happened, O Athenians, that this man appeared to me to be wise in the opinion of many other men, and especially in his own, but that he was not so. And afterwards I endeavored to show him that he fancied himself to be wise, but was not. Hence I became odious to him, and also to many others that were present. Departing, therefore, I reasoned with myself that I was wiser than this man. For it appears that neither of us knows anything beautiful or good; but he, indeed, not knowing, thinks that he knows something; but I, as I do not know anything, neither do I think that I know. Hence in this trifling particular I appear to be wiser than he, because I do not think that I know things which I do not know. After this I went to another of those who appeared to be wiser than he was, and of him also I formed the same opinion. Hence also I became odious to him and many others.

Afterwards, however, I went to others, suspecting and grieving and fearing that I should make enemies. At the same time, however, it appeared to me to be necessary to pay the greatest attention to the oracle of the God, and that, considering what could be its meaning, I should go to all that appeared to possess any knowledge. And by the Dog, O Athenians (for it is necessary to tell you the truth), that which happened to me was as follows: Those that were most celebrated for their wisdom appeared to me to be most remote from it, but others who were considered as far inferior to them possessed more of intellect. But it is necessary to relate to you my wandering, and the labors as it were which I endured, that the oracle might become to me unconfuted. For after the politicians I went to the poets, both tragic and dithyrambic,[1] and also others, expecting that I should here imme-

[1] Dithyrambic poetry was lyric; sung by revellers with flute accompaniment; irregular, like the god Bacchus, in whose honor it was sung.

diately find myself to be less wise than these. Taking up, therefore, some of their poems which appeared to me to be the most elaborately written, I asked them what was their meaning, that at the same time I might learn something from them. I am ashamed, indeed, O Athenians, to tell you the truth, but at the same time it must be told. For, as I may say, all that were present would have spoken better about the things which they had composed. I discovered this, therefore, in a short time concerning the poets, that they did not effect by wisdom that which they did, but by a certain genius and from enthusiastic energy, like prophets and those that utter oracles. For these also say many and beautiful things, but they understand nothing of what they say. Poets, therefore, appear to me to be affected in a similar manner. And at the same time I perceived that they considered themselves, on account of their poetry, to be the wisest of men in other things, in which they were not so. I departed, therefore, also from them, thinking that I surpassed them by the very same thing in which I surpassed the politicians.

In the last place, therefore, I went to the artificers. For I was conscious to myself that I knew nothing, as I may say, but that these men possessed knowledge, because I had found them acquainted with many and beautiful things. And in this, indeed, I was not deceived, for they knew things which I did not, and in this they were wiser than I. But, O Athenians, good artificers also appeared to me to have the same fault as the poets. For each, in consequence of performing well in his art, thought that he was also most wise in other things, and those the greatest. And this their error obscured that very wisdom which they did possess. I therefore asked myself in behalf of the oracle, whether I would choose to be as I am, possessing no part either of their wisdom or ignorance, or to have both which they possess. I answered, therefore, for myself and for the oracle, that it was better for me to be as I am.

From this my investigation, O Athenians, many enmities were excited against me, and such as were most grievous and weighty, so that many calumnies were produced from them; and hence I obtained the appellation of *the wise man*. For those that hear me think that I am wise in these things, the ignorance of which I expose in others. It appears, however, O Athenians, that Divinity is wise in reality, and that in this oracle he says this, that human wisdom[1] is but of little, or indeed of no worth; and it seems that he used my name, making me an example, as if he had said, He, O men, is the wisest among you, who, like Socrates, *knows* that he is in reality of no worth with respect to wisdom. These things, therefore, going about, I even now inquire and explore in obedience to the God, both among citizens and strangers, if any one of them appears to me to be wise; and when I find he is not, giving assistance to the God, I demonstrate that he is not wise. And in consequence of this employment I have no leisure worth mentioning either for public or private transactions; but I am in great poverty through my religious cultivations of the God.

Besides, the youth that spontaneously follow me, who especially abound in leisure, as being the sons of the most wealthy, rejoice on hearing men confuted by me; and often imitating me, they afterwards endeavor to make trial

---

[1] This explains Socrates famous remark "That he knew that he knew nothing" wherein he presents a comparison between human and divine knowledge.

of others. In which attempt I think they find a numerous multitude of men who fancy that they know something, but who know little or nothing. Hence, therefore, those who are tried by them are angry with me, and not with them, and say that there is one Socrates a most wicked person, and who corrupts the youth. And when some one asks them what he does, and what he teaches, they have nothing to say, but are ignorant. That they may not, however, appear to be dubious, they assert things which may be readily adduced against all that philosophize, as, that he explores things on high and under the earth, that he does not think there are gods, and that he makes the worse to appear the better reason. For I think they are not willing to speak the truth, that they clearly pretend to be knowing, but know nothing. Hence, as it appears to me, being ambitious and vehement and numerous, and speaking in a united and plausible manner about me, they fill your ears, calumniating me violently from old time even till now. Among these, Melitus, Anytus, and Lycon, have attacked me; Melitus indeed being my enemy on account of the poets; but Anytus on account of the artificers and politicians; and Lycon on account of the orators. So that, as I said in the beginning, I should wonder if I could remove such an abundant calumny from your minds in so short a time. These things, O Athenians, are true; and I thus speak, neither concealing nor subtracting anything from you, either great or small; though I know well enough that I shall make enemies by what I have said. This, however, is an argument that I speak the truth, that this is the calumny which is raised against me, and that the causes of it are these. And whether now or hereafter you investigate these things, you will find them to be as I have said. Concerning the particulars, therefore, which my first accusers urged against me, let this be a sufficient apology to you.

In the next place, I shall endeavor to reply to Melitus, that good man and lover of his country, as he says, and also to my latter accusers. For again, as being different from the former accusers, let us take their oath also. The accusation then is as follows: SOCRATES, it says, IS AN EVIL-DOER, CORRUPTING THE YOUTH; AND, NOT BELIEVING IN THOSE GODS IN WHICH THE CITY BELIEVES, HE INTRODUCES OTHER NOVEL DÆMONIACAL NATURES. Such then is the accusation; of which let us examine every part. It says, then, that I do evil by corrupting the youth. But I, O Athenians, say that Melitus does evil because he intentionally trifles, rashly bringing men into danger, and pretending to be studious and solicitous about things which were never the objects of his care. But that this is the case I will endeavor to show you.

Tell me then, O Melitus, whether you consider it as a thing of the greatest consequence, for the youth to become the best of men?

I do.

Come, then, do you therefore tell them what will make them better? For it is evident that you know, since it is the object of your care. For, having found me to be a corrupter of youth, as you say, you have brought me hither, and are my accuser; but come, inform me who it is that makes them better, and signify it to this assembly. Do you see, O Melitus, that you are silent, and have not anything to say? Though, does it not appear to you to be shameful, and a sufficient argument of what I say, that this is not the object of your attention? But tell me, O good man, who it is that makes them better?

The laws.

I do not, however, ask this, O best of men, but what man it is that first knows this very thing, the laws.

These men, Socrates, are the judges.

How do you say, Melitus? Do they know how to instruct the youth, and to make them better?

Especially so.

But whether do all of them know how? or do some of them know, and others not?

All of them.

You speak well, by Hera, and adduce a great abundance of those that benefit. But what? Can these auditors also make the youth better, or not?

These also.

And what of the senators?

The senators also can effect this.

But, O Melitus, do some of those that harangue the people in an assembly corrupt the more juvenile; or do all these make them better?

All these.

All the Athenians therefore, as it seems, make them to be worthy and good, except me, but I alone corrupt them. Do you say so?

These very things I strenuously assert.

You charge me with a very great infelicity. But answer me: Does this also appear to you to be the case respecting horses, viz., that all men can make them better, but that there is only one person that spoils them? or does the perfect contrary of this take place, so that it is one person who can make them better, or, at least, that those possessed of equestrian skill are very few; but the multitude, if they meddle with and make use of horses, spoil them? Is not this the case, O Melitus, both with respect to horses and all other animals? It certainly is so, whether you and Anytus say so, or not. For a great felicity would take place concerning youth if only one person corrupted, and the rest benefited them. However, you have sufficiently shown, O Melitus, that you never bestowed any care upon youth; and you clearly evince your negligence, and that you pay no attention to the particulars for which you accuse me.

Further still, tell me, by Zeus, O Melitus, whether it is better to dwell in good or in bad polities? Answer, my friend: for I ask you nothing difficult. Do not the depraved always procure some evil to those that continually reside near them; and do not the good procure some good?[1]

Entirely so.

Is there then any one who wishes to be injured by his associates, rather than to be benefited? Answer, O good man: for the law orders you to answer. Is there any one who wishes to be injured?

There is not.

Come then, whether do you bring me hither, as one that corrupts the youth, and makes them depraved willingly, or as one who does this unwillingly?

I say that you do it willingly.

But what, O Melitus, is it possible that you, who are so much younger than I am, should well know that the depraved always procure some evil to those that are most near to them, and the good some good; but that I should have arrived at such ignorance as not to know that, if I make

---

[1] Influence of environment.

any one of my associates depraved, I shall be in danger of receiving some evil from him; and that I, therefore, do this so great an evil willingly, as you say? I cannot be persuaded by you, O Melitus, as to these things, nor do I think that any other man would: but either I do not corrupt the youth, or I corrupt them unwillingly. So that you speak falsely in both assertions. But if I unwillingly corrupt them, the law does not order me to be brought hither for such-like involuntary offenses, but that I should be taken and privately taught and admonished. For it is evident that, if I am taught better, I shall cease doing that which I unwillingly do. But you, indeed, have avoided me, and have not been willing to associate with and instruct me; but you have brought me hither, where the law orders those who require punishment, and not discipline, to be brought. Wherefore, O Athenians, this now is manifest which I have said, that Melitus never paid the smallest attention to this affair.

At the same time, however, tell us, O Melitus, how you say I corrupt the youth. Or is it not evident, from your written accusation, that I teach them not to believe in the gods in which the city believes, but in other new divine powers? Do you not say that, teaching these things, I corrupt the youth?

Perfectly so: I strenuously assert these things.

By those very gods, therefore, Melitus, of whom we are now speaking, I charge you speak in a still clearer manner both to me and to these men. For I cannot learn whether you say that I teach them to think that there are not certain gods, though I myself believe that there are gods, not being by any means an atheist, nor in this respect an evil-doer—not, indeed, such as the city believes in, but others, and that this it is for which you accuse me, that I introduce other gods; or whether you altogether say that I do not believe there are any gods, and that I teach this doctrine also to others.

I say this, that you do not believe that there are any gods.

O wonderful Melitus, why do you thus speak? Do I then think, unlike the rest of mankind, that the sun and moon are not gods?

He does not, by Zeus, O judges: for he says that the sun is a stone, and that the moon is earth.

O friend Melitus, you think that you accuse Anaxagoras; and you so despise these judges, and think them to be so illiterate, as not to know that the books of Anaxagoras the Clazomenian are full of these assertions. Besides, would the youth learn those things from me, which they might buy for a drachma [nineteen cents] at most in the theatre,[1] and thus might deride Socrates if he pretended they were his own, especially since they are likewise so absurd? But, by Zeus, do I then appear to you to think that there is no God?

None whatever, by Zeus.

What you say, O Melitus, is incredible, and, as it appears to me, is so even to yourself. Indeed, O Athenians, this man appears to me to be perfectly insolent and intemperate in his speech, and to have in reality written this accusation, impelled by a certain insolence, wantonness and youthfulness. For he seems, as it were, to have composed an ænigma in order to try me, and to have said to himself, Will the wise Socrates know that I

---

[1] Euripides, and other dramatists recognized the physical doctrines of Anaxagoras in their dramas.

am jesting, and speaking contrary to myself? Or shall I deceive him, together with the other hearers? For he appears to me to contradict himself in his accusation, as if he had said, Socrates is impious in not believing that there are gods, but believing that there are gods. And this, indeed, must be the assertion of one in jest.

But let us jointly consider, O Athenians, how he appears to me to have asserted these things. And do you, O Melitus, answer us, and, as I requested you at first, be mindful not to disturb me if I discourse after my usual manner. Is there then any man, O Melitus, who thinks that there are human affairs, but does not think that there are men? Pray answer me, and do not make these clamorous digressions. And is there any one who does not think that there are horses, but yet thinks that there are equestrian affairs? or who does not think that there are pipers, but yet that there are things pertaining to pipers? There is not, O best of men. For I will speak for you, since you are not willing to answer yourself. But answer also to this: Is there any one who thinks that there are dæmoniacal affairs, but yet does not think that there are dæmons?

There is not.

How averse you are to speak! so that you scarcely answer, compelled by the judges. Do you not, therefore, say that I believe in and teach things dæmoniacal, whether they are new or old? But indeed you acknowledge that I believe in things dæmoniacal, and to this you have sworn in your accusation. If then I believe in dæmoniacal affairs, there is an abundant necessity that I should also believe in the existence of dæmons. Is it not so? It is. For I suppose you to assent, since you do not answer.

But with respect to dæmons, do we not think either that they are gods, or the sons of gods? Will you acknowledge this or not?

Entirely so.

If, therefore, I believe that there are dæmons as you say, if dæmons are certain gods, will it not be as I say, that you speak ænigmatically and in jest, since you assert that I do not think there are gods, and yet again think that there are, since I believe in dæmons? But if dæmons are certain spurious sons of the gods, either from nymphs, or from certain others, of whom they are said to be the offspring, what man can believe that there are sons of the gods, and yet that there are no gods? For this would be just as absurd as if some one should think that there are colts and mules, but should not think that there are horses and asses. However, O Melitus, it cannot be otherwise but that you have written this accusation, either to try me, or because there was not any crime of which you could truly accuse me. For it is impossible that you should persuade any man who has the smallest degree of intellect, that one and the same person can believe that there are dæmoniacal and divine affairs, and yet that there are neither dæmons, nor gods nor heroes. That I am not, therefore, impious, O Athenians, according to the accusation of Melitus, does not appear to me to require a long apology; but what I have said is sufficient.

As to what I before observed, that there is a great enmity towards me among the vulgar, you may be well assured that it is true. And this it is which will condemn me, if I should happen to be condemned, viz., the hatred and envy of the multitude, and not Melitus, nor Anytus; which indeed has also happened to many others, and those good men, and will, I think, again happen in futurity.[1] For there is no reason to expect that it will terminate in me. Perhaps, however, some one will say, Are you not ashamed, Socrates, to have applied yourself to a study through which you are now in danger of being put to death? To this person I shall justly reply, That you do not speak well, O man, if you think that life or death ought to be regarded by the man who is capable of being useful though but in a small degree; and that he ought not to consider this alone when he acts, whether he acts justly, or unjustly, and like a good or a bad man. For those demigods that died at Troy would, according to your reasoning, be vile characters, as well others as the son of Thetis, who so much despised the danger of death when compared with disgraceful conduct, that when his mother, who was a goddess, on his desiring to kill Hector, thus I think addressed him[2]—My son, if you revenge the slaughter of your friend Patroclus, and kill Hector, you will yourself die, for, said she, death awaits you as soon as Hector expires:—Notwithstanding this, he considered the danger of death as a trifle, and much more dreaded living basely, and not revenging his friends. For he says, May I immediately die, when I have inflicted just punishment on him who has acted unjustly, and not stay here by the curved ships an object of ridicule, and a burden to the ground? Do you think that he was solicitous about death and danger? For this, O Athenians, is in reality the case: wherever anyone ranks himself, thinking it to be the best for him, or wherever he is ranked by the ruler,

---

[1] Is not the condemnation of the ignorant more to be dreaded than that of the educated?

[2] Iliad. Book xviii, verse 94 seq.

there, as it appears to me, he ought to abide, and encounter danger, neither regarding death nor anything else before that which is base.

I therefore, O Athenians, should have acted in a vile manner, if, when those rulers which you had placed over me had assigned me a rank at Potidæa, at Amphipolis, and at Delium,[1] I should then have remained where they stationed me, like any other man, and should have encountered the danger of death; but that, when Divinity has ordered, as I think and apprehend, that I ought to live philosophising, and exploring myself and others, I should here, through fear of death, or any other thing, desert my rank. For this would be vile: and then in reality any one might justly bring me to a court of judicature, and accuse me of not believing in the gods, in consequence of not obeying the oracle, fearing death, and thinking myself to be wise when I am not. For to dread death, O Athenians, is nothing else than to appear to be wise, without being so: since it is for a man to appear to know that which he does not know. For no one knows but that death may be to man the greatest of goods; but they dread it, as if they well knew that it is the greatest of evils. And how is it possible that this should not be the most disgraceful ignorance, I mean for a man to imagine that he has a knowledge of that of which he is ignorant? But I, O Athenians, differ perhaps in this from the multitude of men; and if I should say that I am wiser than some one in anything, it would be in this, that not having a sufficient knowledge of the things in Hades, I also think that I have not this knowledge. But I know that to act unjustly, and to be disobedient to one more

---

[1] Places of three noted battles in Grecian history.

excellent, whether god or man, is evil and base. I shall never, therefore, fear and avoid things which for aught I know may be good, before those evils which I know to be evils. So that neither if you should now dismiss me (being unpersuaded by Anytus, who said that either I ought not to have been brought hither at first, or that, when brought hither, it was impossible not to put me to death, telling you that if I escaped, all your sons studying what Socrates had taught them would be corrupted), if besides these things you should say to me, O Socrates, we now indeed shall not be persuaded by Anytus, but we shall dismiss you, though on this condition, that afterwards you no longer busy yourself with this investigation, nor philosophise, and if hereafter you are detected in so doing, you shall die,—if, as I said, you should dismiss me on these terms, I should thus address you: O Athenians, I honor and love you: but I obey Divinity rather than you; and as long as I breathe and am able, I shall not cease to philosophise, and to exhort and indicate to any one of you I may happen to meet, such things as the following, after my usual manner: O best of men, since you are an Athenian, of a city the greatest and the most celebrated for wisdom and strength, are you not ashamed of being attentive to the means of acquiring riches, glory and honor in great abundance, but to bestow no care nor any consideration upon prudence[1] and truth, nor how your soul may subsist in the most excellent condition? And if anyone of you should contend with me, and say that these things are the objects of his care, I should not immediately dismiss him, nor depart, but I should interrogate, explore and reason with him. And if he should

---

[1] Meaning contemplation of matters pertaining to the intellect.

not appear to me to possess virtue, and yet pretend to the possession of it, I should reprove him as one who but little esteems things of the greatest worth, but considers things of a vile and abject nature as of great importance. In this manner I should act by any one I might happen to meet, whether younger or older, a stranger or a citizen; but rather to citizens, because ye are more allied to me. For be well assured that Divinity commands me thus to act. And I think that a greater good never happened to you in the city, than this my obedience to the will of Divinity. For I go about doing nothing else than persuading both the younger and older among you, neither to pay attention to the body, nor to riches, nor anything else prior to the soul; nor to be so much concerned for anything, as how the soul may subsist in the most excellent condition. I also say that virtue is not produced from riches, but riches from virtue, as likewise all other human goods, both privately and publicly. If, therefore, asserting these things, I corrupt the youth, these things will be noxious; but if any one says that I assert other things than these, he says what is untrue. In addition to this I shall say, O Athenians, that whether you are persuaded by Anytus or not, and whether you dismiss me or not, I shall not act otherwise, even though I should die for it many times.

Be not disturbed, O Athenians, but patiently hear what I shall request of you; for I think it will be advantageous for you to hear. For I am about to mention certain other things to you, at which perhaps you will be clamorous; though let this on no account take place. Be well assured then, if you put me to death, being such a man as I say I am, you will not injure me more than yourselves. For neither Melitus nor Anytus injures me; for neither can they. Indeed, I think it is not possible for a better to be injured by a worse man. He may indeed perhaps condemn me to death, or exile or disgrace; and he or some other may consider these as mighty evils. I however do not think so; but, in my opinion, it is much more an evil to act as he now acts, who endeavors to put a man to death unjustly. Now, therefore, O Athenians, it is far from my intention to defend myself (as some one may think), but I thus speak for your sake, lest in condemning me you should sin against the gift of Divinity. For, if you should put me to death, you will not easily find such another (though the comparison is ridiculous) whom Divinity has united to this city as to a great and generous horse, but sluggish through his magnitude, and requiring to be excited by some gadfly. In like manner Divinity appears to have united such a one as I am to the city, that I might not cease exciting, persuading and reproving each of you, and everywhere lighting upon you through the whole day. Such another man will not easily arise among you. And if you will be persuaded by me, you will spare me. Perhaps, however, you, being indignant, like those who are awakened from sleep, will repulse me, and, being persuaded by Anytus, will inconsiderately put me to death. Should this be the case, you will pass the rest of your time in sleep, unless Divinity should send some other person to take care of you. But that I am such a one as I have said, one imparted to this city by Divinity, you may understand from hence. For my conduct does not appear to be human, in neglecting everything pertaining to myself and my private affairs for so many years, and always attending to your concerns, addressing each of you separately, like a father, or an elder brother, and persuading you to the study of virtue. And if indeed I had obtained any emolument from this conduct, and receiving a recompense had exhorted you to these things, there might be some reason for asserting that I acted like other men; but now behold, even my accusers themselves, who have so shamelessly calumniated me in everything else, have not been so impudent as to charge me with this, or to bring witnesses to prove that I ever either demanded or solicited a reward. And that I speak the truth, my poverty I think affords a sufficient testimony.

Perhaps, therefore, it may appear absurd, that, going about and involving myself in a multiplicity of affairs, I should privately advise these things, but that I should never dare to come to your public assembly, and consult for the city. The cause of this is that which you have often heard me everywhere asserting—viz., because a certain divine and dæmoniacal voice is present with me, which also Melitus in his accusation derided. This voice attended me from a child; and when it is present, always *dissuades* me from what I intended to do, but never *incites* me. This it is which opposed my engaging in political affairs; and to me its opposition appears to be most right and proper. For be well assured, O Athenians, if I had formerly attempted to transact political affairs, I should have perished long before this, and should neither have benefited you in any respect, nor myself. And be not indignant with me for speaking the truth. For it is not possible that any man can be safe, who sincerely opposes either you, or any other multitude, and who prevents many unjust and illegal actions from taking place in the city; but it is necessary that he who will really contend for the right, if he wishes even but for a little to be safe, should live privately, and not engage in public affairs.

I will present you with mighty proofs of these things, not words, but that which you honor more, namely, deeds. Hear then the circumstances which have happened to me, that you may know that I shall not yield to any one contrary to what is becoming, through dread of death; though at the same time by not yielding I should perish. For I, O Athenians, never bore the office of magistrate[1] in the city, but I have been a senator: and it happened that our Antiochean tribe governed, when you thought proper to condemn the ten generals collectively, for not taking up the bodies of those that perished in the naval battle;[2] and in so doing acted illegally, as afterwards appeared to all of you. At that time I alone of the Prytaneans opposed you, that you might not act contrary to the laws, and my suffrage was contrary to yours. When the orators also were ready to point me out and condemn me, and you likewise were exhorting and vociferating to the same end, I thought that I ought rather to encounter danger with law and justice, than adhere to you in your injustice, through fear of bonds or death. And these things indeed happened while the city was yet a democracy; but when it became an oligarchy, the Thirty sent for me and four others to the Tholus, and ordered us to bring Leon the Salaminian from Salamis, in order

---

[1] In 509 B. C., by the reforms of Clisthenes, the Athenians were divided into ten tribes. Fifty men, called Prytani or Senators, were chosen from each tribe, and each set of fifty governed for thirty-five days.

[2] Victory of the ten Athenian generals over the Spartans led by Callicratides, battle of Arginusæ. Latter part of Peloponnesian war.

to be put to death; for by these orders they meant to involve many others in guilt. Then indeed I, not in words but in deeds, showed them, if I may use so vulgar an expression, that I cared not a snap of my fingers for death; but that all my attention was directed to this, that I might do nothing unjust or unholy. For that dominion of the Thirty, though so strong, did not terrify me into the perpetration of any unjust action. But when we departed from the Tholus, the four indeed went to Salamis, and brought with them Leon; but I returned home. And perhaps for this I should have been put to death, if that government had not been rapidly dissolved. These things many of you can testify.

Do you think, therefore, that I could have lived for so many years, if I had engaged in public affairs, and had acted in a manner becoming a good man, giving assistance to justice, and doing this in the most eminent degree? Far otherwise, O Athenians: for neither could any other man. But I, through the whole of my life, if I do anything publicly, shall appear to be such a man; and being the same privately, I shall never grant anything to any one contrary to justice, neither to any other, nor to any one of these whom my calumniators say are my disciples. I however was never the preceptor of any one; but I never repulsed either the young or the old, that were desirous of hearing me speak after my usual manner. Nor do I discourse when I receive money, and refrain from speaking when I do not receive any; but I similarly offer myself to be interrogated by the rich and the poor: and if any one is willing to answer, he hears what I have to say. Of these too, whether any one becomes good or not, I cannot justly be said to be the cause, because I never either promised or taught them any discipline. But if any one says that he has ever learnt or heard anything from me privately, which all others have not, be well assured that he does not speak the truth.

Why therefore some have delighted to associate with me for a long time ye have heard, O Athenians. I have told you all the truth, that men are delighted on hearing those interrogated who think themselves to be wise, but who are not: for this is not unpleasant. But, as I say, I am ordered to do this by Divinity, by oracles, by dreams, and by every mode by which any other divine destiny ever commanded anything to be done by man. These things, O Athenians, are true, and might easily be confuted if they were not. For if, with respect to the youth, I corrupt some, and have corrupted others, it is fit, if any of them have become old, that, knowing that I gave them bad advice when they were young, they should now rise up, accuse and take vengeance on me; but if they themselves are unwilling to do this, that their fathers, or brothers or others of their kindred, should now call to mind and avenge the evil which their relatives suffered from me. But in short, many of them are here present, whom I see:—In the first place, Crito, who is of the same age and city that I am, and who is the father of this Critobulus: in the next place, Lysanias the Sphecian, the father of this Æschines; and further still, Antipho the Cephisian, the father of Epigenes. There are also others whose brothers are in this assembly—viz., Nicostratus, the son of Zotidas, and the brother of Theodotus. And Theodotus indeed is dead, and so will not hinder him. Paralus also is here, the son of Demodochus, of whom Theages was the brother; likewise Adimantus, the son of

Aristo, the brother of whom is this Plato; and Æantidorus, of whom Apollodorus is the brother. I could also mention many others, some one of whom Melitus, especially in his oration, ought to have adduced as a witness. If however he then forgot to do so, let him now produce him, for he has my consent; and if he has anything of this kind to disclose, let him declare it. However, you will find the very contrary of this to be the case, and that all these are ready to assist me who have corrupted and injured their kindred, as Melitus and Anytus say. It might indeed perhaps be reasonable to suppose that those whom I have corrupted would assist me; but what other reason can the relatives of these have, who are not corrupted, and who are now advanced in age, for giving me assistance, except that which is right and just? For they know that Melitus lies, and that I speak the truth. Be it so then, O Athenians: and these indeed, and perhaps other such-like particulars, are what I have to urge in my defense.

Perhaps, however, some one among you will be indignant on recollecting that he, when engaged in a much less contest than this, suppliantly implored the judges with many tears; that he also brought his children hither, that by these he might especially excite compassion, together with many others of his relatives and friends: but I do none of these things, though, as it may appear, I am brought to extreme danger. Perhaps, therefore, some one thus thinking may become more hostile towards me, and, being enraged with these very particulars, may give his vote with anger. If then any one of you is thus affected,—I do not think there is any one, but if there should be, I shall appear to myself to speak equitably to such a one by saying that I also, O best of men, have certain relatives. For, as Homer says, I am not sprung from an oak, nor from a rock, but from men. So that I also, O Athenians, have relations, and three sons; one now a lad; but the other two, boys: I have not however brought any one of them hither, that I might supplicate you on that account to acquit me. Why is it then that I do none of these things? It is not, O Athenians, because I am contumacious, nor is it in contempt of you. And as to my fearing or not fearing death, that is another question. But it does not appear to me to be consistent either with my own credit or yours, or that of the whole city, that I should do anything of this kind at my age, and with the reputation I have acquired, whether true or false. For it is admitted that Socrates surpasses in something the multitude of mankind. If, therefore, those among you who appear to excel either in wisdom, in fortitude or any other virtue, should act in such a manner as I have seen some when they have been judged, it would be shameful: for these, appearing indeed to be something, have conducted themselves very strangely, thinking they should suffer something dreadful by dying, as if they would be immortal if you did not put them to death. These men, as it appears to me would so disgrace the city, that any stranger might apprehend that such of the Athenians as excel in virtue, and who are promoted to the magistracy and other honors in preference to the rest, are no better than women. For these things, O Athenians, ought not to be done by us who have gained some degree of reputation, nor should you suffer us to do them, if we were willing; but you should show that you will much sooner condemn him who introduces these lamentable dramas, and who thus makes the city ridiculous, than him who quietly expects your decision.

But exclusive of our credit, O Athenians, neither does it appear to me to be just for the accused to entreat his judge nor to supplicate for an acquittal; but in my opinion he ought to teach and persuade him. For a judge does not sit for the purpose of showing favor, but that he may judge what is just: and he takes an oath that he will not show favor to any, but that he will judge according to the laws. Hence it is neither fit that we should accustom you, nor that you should be accustomed to forswear yourselves: for in so doing neither of us will act piously. Do not, therefore, think, O Athenians, that I ought to act in such a manner towards you that I should neither conceive to be honorable, nor just nor holy; and especially, by Zeus, since I am accused of impiety by this Melitus. For it clearly follows, that if I should persuade you, and, though you have taken an oath, force you to be favorable, I might then indeed teach that you do not think there are gods; and in reality, while making my defense, I should accuse myself as not believing in the gods. This however is far from being the case: for I believe that there are gods more than any one of my accusers; and I refer it to you and to Divinity to judge concerning me such things as will be best both for me and you.

> After Socrates had thus spoken, votes were taken by the judges, and he was condemned by a majority of five or six voices. His speech after his condemnation commences in the paragraph immediately following.

That I should not, therefore, O Athenians, be indignant with you because you have condemned me, there are many reasons, and among others this, that it has not happened to me contrary to my expectation; but I much rather wonder that there should have been so great a number of votes on both sides. For I did not think that I should have wanted such a few additional votes for my acquittal. But now, as it seems, if only three votes had changed sides, I should have escaped condemnation. Indeed, as it appears to me, I now have escaped Melitus; and I have not only escaped him, but it is perfectly evident that unless Anytus and Lyco had risen to accuse me, he had lost his thousand[1] drachmas, since he had not had the fifth part of the votes on his side.

Melitus then thinks that I deserve death. Be it so. But what punishment,[2] O Athenians, shall I assign to myself? Is it not evident that it will be such a one as I deserve? What then do I deserve to suffer or to pay, for not having during my life concealed what I have learned, but neglected all that the multitude esteem, riches, domestic concerns, military commands, authority in public assemblies and other magistracies? for having avoided the conspiracies and seditions which have happened in the city, thinking that I was in reality a more worthy character than to depend on these things for my safety? I have not, therefore, applied myself to those pursuits, by which

---

[1] According to the law of Athens if there were not one-fifth of the votes in favor of the accusation, the accused was fined a thousand drachmas.

[2] When the criminal was found guilty and the accuser demanded a sentence of death, the law allowed the prisoner to condemn himself to one of these three punishments—viz., perpetual imprisonment, a fine or banishment. This privilege was first enacted on the behalf of the judges, that they might not hesitate to pass sentence on those who, by condemning themselves, owned their guilt. Socrates, therefore, in obedience to the laws, and in order to proclaim his innocence, instead of a punishment demanded a reward worthy of himself.

I could neither benefit you nor myself; but my whole endeavor has been to benefit every individual in the greatest degree; striving to persuade each of you, that he should pay no attention to any of his concerns, prior to that care of himself by which he may become a most worthy and wise man; that he should not attend to the affairs of the city prior to the city itself; and that attention should be paid to other things in a similar manner. What then, being such a man, do I deserve to suffer? Some kind of good, O Athenians, if in reality you honor me according to my desert; and this such a good as it is proper for me to receive. What then is the good which is adapted to a poor man who is a benefactor, and who requires leisure that he may exhort you to virtue? There is not anything more adapted, O Athenians, than that such a man should be supported at the public expense in the Prytaneum; and this much more than if some one of you had been victorious in the Olympic games with horses, or in the two or four-yoked car. For such a one makes you *appear* to be happy, but I cause you *to be* so: and he is not in want of support, but I am. If, therefore, it is necessary that I should be honored according to what is justly my desert, I should be honored with this support in the Prytaneum.

Perhaps, therefore, in saying these things, I shall appear to you to speak in the same manner as when I reprobated lamentations and supplications. A thing of this kind, however, O Athenians, is not the case, but rather the following. I am determined not to injure any man willingly; though I shall not persuade you of this, because the time in which we can discourse with each other is but short. For if there was the same law with you as with others, that in cases of death the judicial process should not continue for one day only but for many, I think I should be able to persuade you. But now it is not easy in a short time to dissolve great calumnies. Being, however, determined to injure no one, I shall be very far from injuring myself, and of pronouncing against myself that I am worthy of evil and punishment. What then? Fearing lest I should suffer that which Melitus thinks I deserve, which I say I know not whether it is good or evil; that I may avoid this, shall I choose that which I well know not to be evil, and think that I deserve this? Whether then shall I choose bonds? But why is it necessary that I should live in prison, in perpetual subjection to the eleven magistrates? Shall I pay a fine then, and remain in bonds till it is discharged? But this is what I just now said: for I have not money to pay it. Shall I then choose exile? For perhaps I shall be thought worthy of this. I should, however, O Athenians, be a great lover of life, if I were so absurd as not to be able to infer that if you, being my fellow-citizens, could not endure my habits and discourses, which have become to you so burdensome and odious, that you now seek to be liberated from them, it is not likely that others would easily bear them. It is far otherwise, O Athenians. My life would be beautiful indeed were I at this advanced age to live in exile, changing and being driven from one city to another. For I well know that, wherever I may go, the youth will hear me when I discourse, in the same manner as they do here. And if I should repel them, they also would expel me, persuading the more elderly to this effect. But if I should not repel them, the fathers and kindred of these would banish me on account of these very young men themselves,

Perhaps, however, some one will say, Can you not, Socrates, live in exile silently and quietly? But it is the most difficult of all things to persuade some among you that this cannot take place. For if I say that in so doing I should disobey Divinity, and that on this account it is impossible for me to live a life of leisure and quiet, you would not believe me, in consequence of supposing that I spoke ironically. And if, again, I should say that this is the greatest good to man, to discourse every day concerning virtue, and other things which you have heard me discussing, exploring both myself and others; and if I should also assert that a life without investigation is not worthy for a man to live, much less, were I thus to speak, would you believe me. These things, however, Athenians, are as I say; but it is not easy to persuade you that they are so. And at the same time I am not accustomed to think myself deserving of any ill. Indeed, if I were rich, I would amerce myself in such a sum as I might be able to pay; but now I am not in a condition to do this, unless you would allow the fine to be proportioned to what I am able to pay. For thus perhaps I might be able to pay a mina of silver [$15.00]. But Plato here, O Athenians, Crito, Critobulus and Apollodorus, exhort me thirty minæ [$450.00], for which they will be answerable. I amerce myself, therefore, in thirty minæ; and these will be my securities for the payment.

> Socrates having amerced himself in obedience to the laws, the judges took the affair into consideration, and, without any regard to the fine, condemned him to die. After the sentence was pronounced, Socrates addressed them as in the next paragraph.

Now, O Athenians, your impatience and precipitancy will draw upon you a great reproach, and give occasion to those who are so disposed, to revile the city for having put that wise man Socrates to death. For those who are willing to reproach you will call me a wise man, though I am not. If, therefore, you had waited but for a short time, this very thing, my death, would have happened to you spontaneously. For behold my age, that it is far advanced in life, and is near to death. But I do not say this to all of you, but to those only who have condemned me to die. This only I say to them: Perhaps you think, O Athenians, that I was condemned through the want of such language, by which I might have persuaded you, if I had thought it requisite to say and do anything, so that I might escape punishment. Far otherwise: for I am condemned through want indeed, yet not of words, but of audacity and impudence, and because I was unwilling to say such things to you as you would have been much gratified in hearing, I at the same time weeping and lamenting, and doing and saying many other things unworthy of me, as I say, but such as you are accustomed to hear and see in others. But neither then did I think it was necessary, for the sake of avoiding danger, to do anything so slavish, nor do I now repent that I have thus defended myself; but I should much rather choose to die, after having made this apology, than to live after that manner. For neither in a judicial process, nor in battle, is it proper that I or any other should devise how he may by any means avoid death; since in battle it is frequently evident that a man might easily avoid death by throwing away his arms, and suppliantly converting himself to his pursuers. There are also many other devices in other dangers, by which he who is ready to do and say anything may escape death. To fly from death, however, O

Athenians, is not difficult, but it is much more difficult to fly from depravity; for it runs swifter than death. And now, I indeed, as being slow and old, am caught by the slower; but my accusers, as being skillful and swift, are caught by the swifter of these two, improbity. Now, too, I indeed depart, condemned by you to death; but they being condemned by truth, depart to depravity and injustice. And I acquiese in this decision, and they also. Perhaps it is necessary that these things should be so, and I think they are right.

In the next place, I desire to predict to you who have condemned me, what will be your fate. For I am now in that situation in which men especially prophesy—viz., when they are about to die. For I say, that you, my murderers, will immediately after my death be punished,[1] in a manner, by Zeus, much more severe than I shall. For now you have done this, thinking you should be liberated from the necessity of giving an account of your life. The very contrary, however, as I say, will happen to you: for many will be your accusers, whom I have restrained, though you did not perceive it. These too will be more troublesome, because they are younger, and will be more indignant against you. For if you think that by putting men to death you will restrain others from upbraiding you that you do not live well, you are much mistaken; since this mode of liberation is neither sufficiently efficacious nor becoming. But this is the most beautiful and the most easy mode, not to disturb others, but to act in

---

[1] This prediction was fulfilled almost immediately after the death of Socrates. The Athenians repented of their cruelty; and his accusers were universally despised and shunned. One of them, Melitus, was torn in pieces; another, Anytus, was expelled the Heraclea, to which he fled for shelter; and others destroyed themselves. And, in addition to this, a raging plague soon after desolated Athens,

such a manner that you may be most excellent characters. And this much I prophesy to those of you who condemned me.

But to you who have acquitted me by your decision, I would willingly speak concerning this affair during the time that the magistrates are at leisure, and before I am brought to the place where I am to die. Attend to me, therefore, O Athenians, during that time. For nothing hinders our conversing with each other as long as we are permitted so to do; since I wish to demonstrate to you, as friends, the meaning of that which has just now happened to me. To me, then, O my judges (and in calling you judges I rightly denominate you), a certain wonderful circumstance has happened. For the prophetic voice of the dæmon, which opposed me in the most trifling affairs, if I was about to act in anything improperly, prior to this, I was continually accustomed to hear; but now, though these things have happened to me which you see, and which some one would think to be the extremity of evils, yet neither when I departed from home in the morning was the signal of the God averse to me, nor when I ascended hither to the place of judgment, nor when I was about to speak,—though at other times it frequently restrained me in the midst of speaking. But now, in this affair, it has never been averse to me either in word or deed. I will now, therefore, tell you what I apprehend to be the cause of this. For this thing which has happened appears to me to be good; nor do those of us apprehend rightly who think death to be an evil; of which this appears to me to be a great argument, that the accustomed signal would have opposed me, unless I had been about to do something good.

After this manner too we may conceive that there is abundant hope that death is good. For to die is one of two things. For it is either to be as it were nothing, and to be deprived of all sensation; or, as it is said, it is a certain mutation and migration of the soul from this to another place. And whether no sensation remains, but death is like sleep when unattended with any dreams, in this case death will be a gain. For, if any one compares such a night as this, in which he so profoundly sleeps as not even to see a dream, with the other nights and days of his life, and should declare how many he had passed better and more pleasantly than this night, I think that not only a private man, but even the Great King himself, would find so small a number that they might be easily counted. If, therefore, death is a thing of this kind, I say it is a gain: for thus the whole of future time appears to be nothing more than one night. But if again death is a migration from hence to another place, and the assertion is true that all the dead are there, what greater good, O my judges, can there be than this. For if some one arriving at Hades, being liberated from these who pretend to be judges, should find those who are true judges, and who are said to judge there—viz., Minos and Rhadamanthus, Æacus and Triptolemus, and such others of the demi-gods as lived justly, would this be a journey to despise? At what rate would you not purchase a conference with Orpheus and Musæus, with Hesiod and Homer? I indeed should be willing to die often if these things are true. For to me the association will be admirable, when I shall meet with Palamedes, and Ajax, the son of Telamon, and any other of the ancients who died through an unjust decision. The comparing my case with theirs will, I think, be no unpleasing employment to me. But the greatest pleasure will consist in passing my time there, as I have done here, in interrogating and exploring who among them is wise, and who fancies himself to be but is not so. What, O my judges, would not any one give for a conference with him who led that mighty army against Troy, or with Odysseus, or Sisyphus, or ten thousand others, both men and women, that might be mentioned? For to converse and associate with these, and interrogate them, would be an inestimable felicity. There, assuredly, it is no capital crime to do so; since they are in other respects more happy than those that live here, and are for the rest of time immortal, if the assertions respecting these things are true.

You, therefore, O my judges, ought to entertain good hopes with respect to death, and to be firmly persuaded of this one thing, that to a good man nothing is evil, neither while living nor when dead, and that his concerns are never neglected by the gods. Nor is my present condition the effect of chance; but this is evident to me, that now to die, and be liberated from the affairs of life, is better for me. On this account the accustomed signal did not in this affair oppose me. Nor am I very indignant with those that accused and condemned me, though their intention in so doing was to injure me; and for this they deserve to be blamed. Thus much, however, I request of them: That you will punish my sons when they grow up, afflicting them as I have afflicted you, if they shall appear to you to pay more attention to riches or anything else than to virtue; and if they shall think themselves to be something when they are nothing, that you will reprobate them as I do you, for neglecting the care of things to which they ought to attend, and conceiving themselves to be of some consequence when they are of no worth. If ye do these things, your conduct both towards me and my sons will be just. But it is now time for us to depart hence,—for me to die, but for you to live. Which of us, however, will arrive at a better thing is manifest to none but Divinity.

INTRODUCTION TO THE PHÆDO.

IN the time of Socrates and Plato, human thought was in its beginning. Man's mind had not reached out and grasped hold of those great ideas of life and death which it afterwards attained.

There were, of course, many instructive feelings about life and death, thoughts, hopes and fears which seem indigenous to all human flesh. Man wondered who he was, whence he came and whither he went. But he only wondered; he had not as yet reasoned much about it.

The time of these two great Greeks was, we might say, the cradle of philosophy.

Immortality is the great lesson of Socrates and Plato. All men have a more or less shadowy notion of some kind of future life.

It is and has been accepted by many, perhaps by most men, merely from some inward prompting of the instinct. But Socrates first, and Plato afterwards, reasoned about this immortality, this life after death, this second life.

The idea of immortality, once accepted without discussion, grew stronger when nurtured by the light of scientific thought. Fearless doubt and inquiry at first led some devout souls to fear for the preservation of such a precious hope. But doubt, inquiry and reason strengthen truth. Doubt and investigation are not always negative in their conclusions. They are more frequently affirmative in their final results. But some will say that immortality is not a thing to be investigated; that which is beyond and after the life of man can not be known by him. Under such difficulties then, as the limitations of man's earthly existence place him, he must resort in his reasoning to methods of analogy. We therefore look to the actions of nature, to the chrysalis and the butterfly and similar phenomena. It would seem that all men who believe in an all powerful, all good God, must simultaneously believe in the eternal life of man. The nature of such a God and the first principles of morality and immortality go hand in hand throughout all eternity. Again, how short is the life of fame! How soon are men forgotten! How few, if any men are really remembered or cared for beyond their own generation! Are such men, mighty souls on earth to fall and be no more forever? If so, life is a farce, a joke, a delusion, a passing fancy, nothing.

The soul is the great ideal. Plato thinks that the soul has a life by itself; Spinoza that the soul vanishes into infinity, that it has no existence by itself. Are soul and body separable or inseparable? If separable, there may be immortality; if inseparable, there is none. The human being alone has the consciousness of truth and justice and love, which is the consciousness of God. The soul becoming more conscious of these, becomes more conscious of its own immortality. (Psalms vi : 5 ; xvi : 10 ; xc ; Isaiah xxxviii: 18 ; Ecclesiastes viii: 8-17 ; iii:19; iv: 2).

But what is immortality? Who receive its blessings? The first we can not answer in any definite way. The thing itself is too indefinite for us to wish any exact description. But let us be content with simply saying that it is life everlasting, somewhere, somehow. But the second ; who receive its blessings? Verily, we could not conceit to ourselves such vast far reaching happiness and deny it to others. The bad have need of it more than the good. Yet we would not refuse it to the good. A wicked man is an object of pity more than of hatred. A great divine mercy is more consistent than anger. Yet it is rather a common feeling that the wicked never see all perfect, immortal happiness. By some, they are condemned to everlasting punishment, or everlasting death. We may in our argument ask ourselves why these men take more delight in cursing the wicked than in uplifting them. But the necessity for such a question carries with it the total lack of any necessity for an answer. The mind of a man who hurls his offending brother into an abyss of constant torture or into an ethereal nothingness, at the same time appropriating to himself perfect eternal happiness, can have no reason but a poisoned, inflammable and biased brain. We may be sure that many such would themselves be wicked, if placed in the circumstances of the wicked. Mercy, pity then lead us to a belief in a universal, not a limited immortality.

Perhaps immortality is a growth in knowledge and in good. All men could participate in such an immortality. Death would then be simply a boundary, marking an epoch of everlasting life, a station in the journey of eternal existence. The world is constantly growing better. It has passed through thousands of years of slow improvement. Its customs, laws, institutions have gone through various stages of development, always changing and progressing for the better. The physical, mental and moral condition of man is better than it ever was. Then let us conjecture that immortality is a part of this vast scheme of growth towards perfection. But let no one dream when that perfection will be reached. We might as well attempt to plan a pedestrian journey to the farthest star and then from that star to each and all the others.

Belief in a perfect God carries with it belief in immortality. A good, wise and merciful all perfect God would not condemn rational beings like ourselves to separation from the immortal happiness of His Own Perfection. Therefore immortality is one and inseparable with an All Perfect God.

ARGUMENT OF THE PHÆDO

PHLIUS. PLACE OF NARRATION.
SCENE. PRISON OF SOCRATES.

PHÆDO, a disciple of Socrates, narrates the dialogue to Echecrates of Phlius. The narration by Phædo took place a year or more after the death of Socrates.

There was a custom in Athens that no punishment by the State should take place while the Sacred Ship was out of the harbor. When Socrates was condemned to death this sacred boat was on a voyage to Delos and return. Thirty days elapsed between the time of Socrates' condemnation and the return of the ship. The philosopher during this interval daily received his friends and discussed as he had always done before, the great things of life and death. On the occasion described by Plato, there were present besides Phædo, the narrator of the story, Simmias and Cebes, from Thebes, Crito, an old friend, Apollodorus, Euclid and others, together with Xantippe, Socrates' famous scolding wife. The latter is first excluded from the company and Socrates and his few chosen friends begin their deliberations.

Socrates begins his argument with a reference to the law of the alternation of opposites as one point of evidence of immortality. When he has spoken along this line a short time, and has reached a climax showing his utter lack of fear of death, Cebes complains of the philosopher's absolute indifference about death. His friends manifest their dislike of his approaching death and Socrates calms them with his anticipation of coming and greater happiness with other gods and friends in death. Life is a prison; when the door is opened, man should be willing to leave and enter the freedom of immortality. Socrates asks; "What is death?" He answers: "It is the separation of soul and body." He desires to escape from the prison of the body, from the desires of the senses. He can not see truth clearly when prejudiced by animal interests. He longs for the complete sway of the all absorbing mind, the universal, immortal mind that dwells only on truth. He speaks of the mysteries and quotes "Many are the wand bearers but few are the mystics." ("Many are called but few are chosen."—Matt. xxii: 14.)

But Cebes fears the possibility of the annihilation of the soul with the death of the body. Socrates refutes this by the doctrine of opposites; sleeping, waking; good, bad; life, death. Life is generated from death. Nature proves this in many ways. Plant life is a notable example.

Another argument brought out in the discussion is that reminiscence proves the pre-existence of the soul. There is in an untutored youth an inherent knowledge of mathematics. The association of ideas and pictures is another. Simmias and Cebes say these things prove only a former existence. Socrates speaks of the soul as indissoluble, as the body is dissoluble. The invisible idea and the visible object of sense are as the immortality of the soul, and the mortality of the body. The soul is the image of divinity.

But perhaps polluted, debased souls may pass into the rougher, more sluggish animals; the virtuous but not philosophical into gentle animals, and philosophers go to gods. However that may be, Socrates has learned not to care about pleasure and pain. He is calm in search of truth.

Cebes and Simmias ponder over his words. Simmias draws a figure of the lyre and harmony; Cebes, one of a coat and its wearer; comparisons are drawn with the soul and the body. Is the soul the harmony of the body? The pre-existence of ideas and the soul is before the body; it is a cause of it; but harmony is after an instrument; an effect. Socrates does not consider the soul a harmony of the body.

Socrates then draws a lesson from his youth. He had always been puzzled over the growth of things, of generation and destruction. He heard a reading of Anaxagoras, that mind is the cause of all things. This spread new light upon his darkness. He then stoutly maintains that the existence of ideas proves the existence of the soul. He indulges at this point in a learned disquisition on the existence of the soul. He dwells upon the growth of the soul from life to death. His mind expands to dwell upon growth during the course of ages. In closing he cheers his hearers with a happy anticipation of the glories of future existence, for this brings companionship and converse with the gods. He mentions the pagan account of Hades and says he does not literally believe in this description but thinks there will be something like it.

The closing irony about Asclepius is somewhat doubtful in its meaning. Perhaps he meant that death was health.

Throughout the long discussion there runs through all the other arguments the one most powerful, that of the existence of eternal ideas, of which the soul is a partaker. But perhaps the most effective argument for immortality is the great Philosopher's gentleness and willingness to die.

THE PHÆDO.

PERSONS OF THE DIALOGUE.

| ECHECRATES. | SIMMIAS. | CRITO. |
| PHÆDO. | CEBES. | THE JAILER. |

Echecrates. Were you present, Phædo, with Socrates that day when he drank the poison in prison? or did you hear an account of it from any other?

Phædo. I myself, Echecrates, was present.

Echec. What then was his discourse previous to his death? and how did he die? for I should be very glad to hear the account: for scarcely does any one of the Phliasian[1] citizens now visit Athens; and it is some time since any stranger has arrived from thence who might afford us some clear information about these particulars. All indeed that we heard was, that he died through drinking the poison; but he who acquainted us with this had nothing further to say about other particulars of his death.

Phæd. What! did you not hear the manner in which he was tried?

Echec. Yes: a certain person related this to us; and we wondered, as his sentence was passed so long ago, that he should not die till a considerable time after. What, then, Phædo, was the reason of this?

Phæd. A certain fortune happened to him, Echecrates: for, the day before his trial, the stern of that ship was crowned which the Athenians send every year to Delos.

---

[1] Phlius, where Echecrates belonged, was a town of Sicyonia in Peloponnesus.

Echec. But what is the meaning of this?

Phæd. This is the ship, as the Athenians say, in which Theseus formerly carried the twice seven young children[1] to Crete, and saved both them and himself. The Athenians, therefore, as it is reported, then vowed to Apollo, that if the children were preserved, they would send every year a sacred embassy to Delos; which, from that time, they regularly send every year to the God. As soon, therefore, as the preparations for the sacred spectacle commence, the law orders that the city shall be purified, and that no one shall be put to death by a public decree till the ship has arrived at Delos, and again returned to Athens. But this sometimes takes a long time in accomplishing, when the winds impede their passage; but the festival itself commences when the priest of Apollo has crowned the stern of the ship. Now this, as I told you, took place on the day preceding the trial; and on this account that length of time happened to Socrates in prison between his sentence and his death.

Echec. And what, Phædo, were the circumstances respecting his death? what were his sayings and actions? and who of his familiars were present with him? or would not the magistrates suffer that any should be admitted to him, so that he died deprived of the presence of his friends?

Phæd. By no means; but some, and indeed many, were present with him.

Echec. Endeavor to relate all these particulars to us in the clearest manner, unless you have some business which may prevent you.

Phæd. But I am at leisure, and will endeavor to

---

[1] The tribute of victims for the Minotaur, which Theseus slew.

gratify your request: for indeed to call to mind Socrates, whether I myself speak or hear others, is to me always the most pleasant of all things.

Echec. Truly, Phædo, others who hear you will be affected in the same manner: but endeavor, as much as you are able, to narrate every circumstance in the most accurate manner.

Phæd. And indeed I myself, who was present, was wonderfully affected; for I was not influenced with pity, like one present at the death of a familiar: for this man, O Echecrates, appeared to me to be blessed, when I considered his manner and discourses, and his intrepid and generous death. Hence it appeared to me, that he did not descend to *Hades* without a divine destiny, but that there also he would be in a happy condition, if ever man was. On this account I was entirely uninfluenced with pity, though apparently I ought not to have been, on so mournful an occasion; nor yet again was I influenced by pleasure through philosophical converse, as I used to be; for our discourses were of this kind. But, to speak ingenuously, a certain wonderful passion, and an unusual mixture of pleasure and grief, were present with me, produced by considering that he must in a very short time die. And, indeed, all of us who were present were nearly affected in the same manner, at one time laughing, and at another weeping: but this was eminently the case with one of us, Apollodorus; for you know the man, and his manner of behavior.

Echec. How is it possible that I should not?

Phæd. He was remarkably affected in this manner; and I myself, and others, experienced great trouble and confusion.

5

Echec. Who then, Phædo, happened to be present?

Phæd. Of native Athenians, Apollodorus, Critobulus, and his father Crito were present; likewise Hermogenes, Epigenes, Æschines and Antisthenes.[1] And besides these, Ctesippus the Pæanian, Menexenus and some other Athenians were present: but Plato I think was sick.

Echec. Were there no strangers?

Phæd. Yes: Simmias the Theban, Cebes and Phædondes; and among the Megarensians, Euclid and Terpsion.

Echec. But what! were not Aristippus[2] and Cleombrotus there?

Phæd. By no means: for they were said to be at Ægina.

Echec. Was any other person present?

Phæd. I think those I have mentioned were nearly all.

Echec. Will you now then relate what were his discourses?

Phæd. I will endeavor to relate the whole to you from the beginning. For we were always accustomed to visit Socrates, myself and others meeting in the morning at the place where he was tried, for it was very near to the prison. Here we waited every day till the prison was

---

[1] Antisthenes, like Socrates in endurance and contempt of pleasure; a cynic; teacher of Diogenes.

[2] A philosopher of Cyrene, and founder of the Cyrenaic sect. What is here said concerning the absence of Aristippus and Cleombrotus is well explained by Demetrius in his book περὶ Ερμηνείας. "Plato, he observes, says this in order to reprove Aristippus and Cleombrotus, who were feasting in Ægina at the time that Socrates was in prison, and did not sail to see their friend and master, though they were then at the entrance of the Athenian harbor. Plato, however, does not clearly relate these particulars, because his narration would have been an open defamation."

opened, discoursing among ourselves, for it was not opened very early in the morning; but, as soon as we could be admitted, we went to Socrates, and generally spent the whole day with him. And then, indeed, we met together sooner than usual; for the day before, when we left the prison, we heard that the ship from Delos was returned. We determined, therefore, among ourselves, to come very early in the morning to the usual place; and we met together accordingly: but when we arrived, the jailer who used to attend upon us, told us to wait, and not enter till he called us. For, says he, the eleven magistrates are now freeing Socrates from his bonds, and announcing to him that he must die to-day. But not long after this he returned, and ordered us to enter. When we entered, we found Socrates just freed from his fetters, but Xantippe (you know her) holding one of his children, and sitting by him. As soon, therefore, as Xantippe saw us, she began to lament in a most violent manner, and said such things as are usual with women in affliction; and among the rest, Socrates, says she, this is the last time your friends will speak to you, or you to them. But Socrates looking upon Crito, Crito, says he, let some one take her home. Upon which some of Crito's domestics led her away, beating herself, and weeping bitterly. But Socrates, sitting upright on the bed, drew up his leg, and rubbing it with his hand, said at the same time, What a wonderful thing is this, my friends, which men call *the pleasant and agreeable!* and how admirably is it affected by nature towards that which appears to be its contrary, *the painful!* for they are unwilling to be present with us both together; and yet, if any person pursues and receives the one, he is almost under a necessity of receiving the other, as if they were two bodies with a single head. And it seems to me, says he, that if Æsop had perceived this he would have composed a fable from it, and would have informed us, that Divinity, being willing to reconcile contending natures, but not being able to accomplish this design, conjoined their summits in a nature one and the same; and that hence it comes to pass, that whoever partakes of the one is soon after connected with the other. And this, as it appears, is the case with myself at present; for the pain which was before in my leg, through the bond, is now succeeded by a pleasant sensation.

But here Cebes replying, said, By Zeus, Socrates, you have very opportunely caused me to recollect: for certain persons have asked me concerning those poems which you composed—viz., the Fables of Æsop which you versified, and your exordium to Apollo, and other pieces of composition; and, among the rest, Evenus lately inquired with what design you did this after coming here, when before you have never attempted anything of the kind. If, therefore, you have any desire that I may have an answer ready for Evenus, when he again interrogates me on this occasion (and I am certain that he will do so), tell me what I must say to him. You may truly inform him, says he, Cebes, that I did not compose these verses with any design of rivaling him, or his poems (for I knew that this would be no easy matter); but that I might try to explore the meaning of certain dreams, and that I might fulfil my religious obligation, if this should happen to be the music which they have often ordered me to exercise. For in the past part of my life the same dream has often occurred to me, exhibiting at different times a different appearance, yet always advising me the same thing; for it said,

Socrates, make and exercise music. And indeed, in the former part of my life, I considered that this dream persuaded and exhorted me respecting the very thing I was doing, in the same manner as runners in the races are exhorted; for, by persuading me to exercise music, it signified that I should labor in philosophy, which is the greatest music. But now since my sentence has taken place, and the festival of the God has retarded my death, it appeared to me to be necessary that, if the music which the dream has so often exhorted me to undertake should happen to be of the ordinary sort, I should by no means resist its persuasions, but comply with the exhortation: for I considered that it would be more safe for me not to depart from hence before I had cleared myself by composing verses, and obeying the dream. Thus, in the first place, I composed some verses in honor of the God to whom the present festival belongs; but after the God, considering it necessary that he who designs to be a poet should make fables and not discourses, and knowing that I myself was not a mythologist, on these accounts I versified the fables of Æsop, which were at hand, and were known to me; and began with those first that first presented themselves to my view. Give this answer, Cebes, to Evenus: at the same time bid him farewell for me; and tell him, if he is wise he will follow me. But I shall depart, as it seems, to-day; for such are the orders of the Athenians.

Upon this Simmias replied, What is this, Socrates, which you command me to tell Evenus? for I often meet with him; and from what I know of him, I am certain that he will never willingly comply with your request.

What, then, says Socrates, is not Evenus a philosopher?

To me he appears to be so, says Simmias.

Both Evenus, therefore, will be willing to follow me, and every one who is worthy to partake of philosophy; not perhaps indeed by violently depriving himself of life, for this they say is unlawful. And at the same time, as he thus spoke, he withdrew his leg from the bed, and placed it on the ground; and afterwards continued to discourse with us, in a sitting posture, the remaining part of the time. Cebes, therefore, inquired of him, How is this to be understood, Socrates, that it is not lawful to commit suicide, and yet that a philosopher should be willing to follow one who is about to die?

What, says he, Cebes, have not you and Simmias heard your familiar Philolaus[1] discourse concerning things of this kind?

We have not, Socrates, heard anything clearly on this subject.

But I, says Socrates, speak in consequence of having heard; and what I have heard I will not enviously conceal from you. And perhaps it is becoming in the most eminent degree, that he who is about to depart thither should consider and mythologise about this departure: I mean, what kind of a thing we should think it to be. For what else can such a one be more properly employed about, till the setting of the sun?[2]

On what account then, Socrates, says Cebes, do they say that it is unlawful for a man to kill himself? for I myself have some time since heard from Philolaus, when he resided with us, and from some others, that it was not

---

[1] A Pythagorean of Crotona.

[2] The law of Athens forbade the execution of the death penalty in the daytime; with a similar idea the philosophy of Pythagoras forbade any one to sleep in the day when nature, like the sun, should be active and energetic.

proper to commit such an action; but I never heard anything clear upon the subject from any one.

Prepare yourself, then, says Socrates, for perhaps you may be satisfied in this particular: and perhaps it may appear to you wonderful, if this alone should be the absolute truth, that it is better, not for some men only but for all, to die than to live; and yet that these men must not, on pain of impiety, do good to themselves, but await some other benefactor.

Then Cebes, gently laughing, Zeus knows that, says he, speaking in his own Bœotian tongue.

For this indeed, says Socrates, appears to be irrational; and yet, perhaps, it is not so, but has a certain reason on its side. For the discourse which is delivered about these particulars, in the arcana of the mysteries,[1] *that we are placed as in a certain prison secured by a guard, and that it is not proper for any one to free himself from this confinement, and make his escape*, appears to me to be an assertion of great moment, and not easy to be understood. But this appears to me, O Cebes, to be well said, that the gods take care of us, and that we who are men are one of the possessions belonging to the gods. Or does not this appear to you to be the case?

It does to me, says Cebes.

Would not you, therefore, if any one of your servants should destroy himself, when at the same time you did not signify that you were willing he should die, would you not be angry with him? and if you had any punishment, would you not chastise him?

Entirely so, says he.

[1] This passage is generally referred to the Mysteries, from which we have an argument against suicide founded on a mystical doctrine of the divine origin of the body.

Perhaps, therefore, it is not irrational to assert, that a man ought not to kill himself before Divinity lays him under a certain necessity of doing so, such as I am subject to at present.

This, indeed, says Cebes, appears to be reasonable. But that which you said just now, Socrates, that philosophers would very readily be willing to die, appears to be absurd, if what we have asserted is agreeable to reason, that Divinity takes care of us, and that we are one of his possessions; for it is irrational to suppose that the wisest men should not be grieved, when departing from that servitude in which they are taken care of by the gods, who are the best of governors. For such a one will by no means think that he shall be better taken care of when he becomes free: but some one who is deprived of intellect may perhaps think that he should fly from his master, and will not consider that he ought not to fly from a good master, but that he should by all means abide in his service. Hence he will depart from him in a most irrational manner: but he who is endowed with intellect will desire to live perpetually with one who is better than himself. And thus, Socrates, it is reasonable that the contrary of what you just now said should take place: for it is proper that the wise, when about to die, should be sorrowful, but that the foolish should rejoice.

Socrates upon hearing this, seemed to me to be pleased with the reasoning of Cebes; and looking upon us, Cebes, says he, never suffers anything to pass without investigation, and is by no means willing to admit immediately the truth of an assertion.

But indeed, says Simmias, Cebes, O Socrates, appears to me to say something now to the purpose. For with what design can men, truly wise, fly from masters who are better than themselves, and, without any reluctance, free themselves from their servitude? And Cebes appears to me to direct his discourse to you, because you so easily endure to leave us, and those beneficent rulers the gods, as you yourself confess.

You speak justly, says Socrates; for I think you mean that I ought to make my defense, as if I was upon my trial.

By all means, says Simmias.

Be it so then, says Socrates: and I shall endeavor that this my apology may appear more reasonable to you than the other did to my judges. For, with respect to myself, says he, O Simmias and Cebes, unless I thought that I should depart, in the first place, to other[1] gods who are wise and good, and, in the next place, to men who have migrated from the present life, and are better than any among us, it would be wrong not to be troubled at death: but now believe for certain, that I hope to dwell with good men; though this, indeed, I will not confidently assert: but that I shall go to gods who are perfectly good rulers, you may consider as an assertion which, if anything of the kind is so, will be strenuously affirmed by me. So that, on this account, I shall not be afflicted at dying, but shall entertain a good hope that something remains for the dead; and, as it was formerly said, that it will be much better hereafter for the good than the evil.

What, then, Socrates, says Simmias, would you have departed with such a conception in your intellect, without communicating it to us? Or will you not render us also

---

[1] By *other gods*, Socrates means such as are of an order superior to the ruling divinities of the world. In short, those gods are here signified that are unconnected with the body.

partakers of it? For it appears to me, that this will be a common good; and at the same time it will be an apology for you, if you can persuade us to believe what you say.

I will endeavor to do so, says he. But let us first attend to Crito: what is that he has for some time seemed anxious to say to me?

What else, says Crito, should it be, Socrates, except what he who is to give you the poison has long ago told me, that you ought to speak as little as possible? For he says that those who dispute become too much heated, and that nothing of this kind ought to be introduced with the poison, since those who do not observe this caution are sometimes obliged to drink the poison twice or thrice.

Let him, says Socrates, only mind his business, and administer the poison twice; and even, if occasion requires, thrice.

I was almost certain, says Crito, that this would be your answer; but he has been plaguing me to do this, as I said, some time since.

Let him be, says Socrates; but I am desirous of rendering to you, as my judges, the reason, as it appears to me, why a man who has truly passed his life in the exercise of philosophy should with great propriety be confident when about to die, and should possess good hopes of obtaining the greatest advantages after death; and in what manner this takes place I will endeavor, Simmias and Cebes, to explain:

Those who are conversant with philosophy in a proper manner, seem to have concealed from others that the whole of their study is nothing else than how to die and be dead.¹ If this then is true, it would certainly be absurd that those who have made this alone their study through the whole of life, should, when it arrives, be afflicted at a circumstance upon which they have before bestowed all their attention and labor.

But here Simmias laughing, By Zeus, says he, Socrates, you cause me to laugh, though I am very far from desiring to do so at present: for I think that the multitude, if they heard this, would consider it as well said against philosophers; and that men of the present day would perfectly agree with you, that philosophers should in reality desire death, and that our fellow-citizens are by no means ignorant that they deserve it.

And indeed, Simmias, they would speak the truth, except in asserting that they are not ignorant of it: for both the manner in which true philosophers desire to die, and how they are worthy of death, is concealed from them. But let us bid farewell to such as these, says he, and discourse among ourselves: and to begin, Do you think that death is anything?

Simmias replied, Entirely so.

Is it anything else than a liberation of soul from body? and is not this to die,² for the body to be liberated from the soul, and to subsist apart by itself? and likewise for the soul to be liberated from the body, and to be essentially separate. Is death anything else but this?

[1] It has been well observed that *to die* differs from *to be dead*. For the cathartic philosopher *dies* in consequence of meditating death; but the theoretic philosopher is *dead*, in consequence of being separated from the passions.

[2] The following is taken from Taylor: "Plato beautifully defines death to be a separation of the body from the soul, and of the soul from the body. For, with respect to souls that are enamored with body, the body is indeed separated from the soul, but not the soul from the body, because it is yet conjoined with it through habitude or alliance, from which those shadowy phantoms are produced that wander about sepulchres."

It is no other, says Simmias.

Consider then, excellent man, whether the same things appear to you as to me; for from hence I think we shall understand better the subjects of our investigation. Does it appear to you that the philosopher is a man who is anxiously concerned about things which are called pleasures, such as meats and drinks?

Not at all, Socrates, says Simmias.

But what about the pleasures of love—does he care for them?

By no means.

Or does such a man appear to you to esteem other particulars which regard the observance of the body, such as the acquisition of excellent garments and sandals, and other ornaments of the body? whether does he appear to you to esteem or despise such particulars, employing them only so far as an abundant necessity requires?

A true philosopher, says Simmias, appears to me to be one who will despise everything of this kind.

Does it, therefore, appear to you, says Socrates, that the whole employment of such a one will not consist in things which regard the body, but in separating himself from the body as much as possible, and in converting himself to his soul?

It does appear so to me.

Is it not, therefore, first of all evident, in things of this kind, that a philosopher, in a manner far surpassing other men, separates his soul in the highest degree from communion with the body?

It appears so.

And to *the many*, O Simmias, it appears that for him who accounts nothing of this kind pleasant, and who does not partake of them, it is not worth while to live; but that he nearly approaches to death who is not concerned about the pleasures of the body.

You entirely speak the truth.

But what with respect to the acquisition[1] of wisdom? Is the body an impediment or not, if any one associates it in the investigation of wisdom? What I mean is this: Have sight and hearing in men any truth?[2] or is the case such as the poets perpetually sing, that

> We nothing accurate or see or hear?

Though if these senses are neither accurate nor clear, by no means can the rest be so: for all the others are in a certain respect more depraved than these. Or does it not appear so to you?

Entirely so, says he.

When then does the soul touch upon the truth? for, when it endeavors to consider anything in conjunction with the body, it is evidently then deceived by the body.

You speak the truth.

Must not, therefore, something of reality become manifest to the soul in the energy of reasoning, if this is ever the case?

It must.

But the soul then reasons best when it is disturbed by nothing belonging to the body, neither by hearing, nor sight, nor pain nor any pleasure, but subsists in the most

---

[1] Socrates having shown from *life* that the philosopher is willing to *die*, now proves this from *knowledge* as follows: The philosopher despises the senses: he who does this depises also the body, in which the senses reside: he who despises the body is averse to it: he who is averse to it separates himself from the body: and he who separates himself from the body is willing to die; for death is nothing else than a separation of the soul from the body.

[2] Plato says that there is no truth in the senses, because they do not properly know.

eminent degree, itself by itself, bidding farewell to the body, and, as much as possible, neither communicating nor being in contact with it, extends itself towards real being?

These things are so.

Does not the soul of a philosopher, therefore, in these employments, despise the body in the most eminent degree, and, flying from it, seek to become essentially subsisting by itself?

It appears so.

But what shall we say, Simmias, about such things as the following? Do we say that the *just itself*[1] is something or nothing?

By Zeus, we say it is something.

And do we not also say, that the *beautiful* and the *good* are each of them something?

How is it possible we should not?

But did you ever at any time behold any one of these with your eyes?

By no means, says he.

But did you ever touch upon these with any other corporeal sense (but I speak concerning all of them; as for instance, about magnitude, health, strength, and, in one word, about the essence of all the rest, and which each truly possesses)? Is then the most true nature of these perceived through the ministry of the body? or rather shall

---

[1] Socrates having shown that the philosopher is willing to die, because he flies from the body, despising it; and having also shown this because he attends to the body no further than extreme necessity obliges him; he now also shows that he is willing to die, from a conversion to things more excellent. For he wishes to know ideas; but it is impossible for the soul to know these while energising with the body, or having this communicating with it in the investigation of them. If this then be the case, the soul will not receive, as its associate in investigation, either the body or the senses, or the instruments of sense, if it wishes to know things accurately.

we not say, that whoever among us prepares himself to think dianoëtically [intellectually] in the most eminent and accurate manner about each particular object of his speculation, such a one will come nearest to the knowledge of each?

Entirely so.

Will not he, therefore, accomplish this in the most pure manner, who in the highest degree betakes himself to each through his dianoëtic power, neither employing sight in conjunction with the dianoëtic energy, nor bringing in any other sense, together with his reasoning; but who, exercising a pure dianoëtic energy as it subsists, at the same time endeavors to hunt after everything which has true being by itself separate and pure; and who in the most eminent degree is liberated from the eyes and ears, and in short from the whole body, as disturbing the soul, and not suffering it to acquire truth and wisdom by its conjunction? Will not such a man, Simmias, procure for himself real being, if this can ever be asserted of any one?

You speak the truth, Socrates, says Simmias, in a transcendent manner.

Is it not necessary, therefore, says Socrates, from hence, that an opinion of this kind should be present with genuine philosophers in such a manner, that they will speak among themselves as follows: In the consideration of things, this opinion, like a kind of path, leads us in conjunction with reason from the vulgar track, that, as long as we are connected with a body, and our soul is contaminated with such an evil, we can never sufficiently obtain the object of our desire; and this object we have asserted to be truth? For the body subjects us to innumerable occupations through necessary aliment, and fills us with love, desire, fear, all various images, and a multitude of trifling concerns; not to mention that, if we are invaded by certain diseases, we are hindered by them in our hunting after real being; so that, as it is said, *we can never truly, and in reality, acquire wisdom through the body.* For nothing else but the body and its desires cause wars, seditions and contests of every kind: for all wars arise through the possession of wealth; and we are compelled to acquire riches through the body, becoming subservient to its cultivation; so that on all these accounts we have no leisure for the exercise of philosophy. But this is the extremity of all evils, that if at any time we are at leisure from its attendance, and betake ourselves to the speculation of anything, then invading us on all sides in our investigations, it causes agitations and tumults, and so vehemently impels us, that we are not able through its presence to perceive the truth; but it is in reality demonstrated to us, that, if we are designed to know anything purely, we must be liberated from the body, and behold things with the soul itself. And then, as it appears, we shall obtain the object of our desire, and of which we profess ourselves lovers—viz., wisdom, when we are dead, as our discourse evinces; but by no means while we are alive: for, if we can know nothing purely in conjunction with the body, one of these two consequences must ensue, either that we can never possess knowledge, or that we must obtain it after death; for then the soul will subsist apart by itself, separate from the body, but never before this takes place; and while we live in the body, as it appears, we shall approach in the nearest manner possible to knowledge, if in the most eminent degree we have no association with the body, nor any communication with it (except what the greatest necessity requires), nor are filled with its nature, but purify ourselves from its defiling connection, till Divinity itself dissolves our bonds. And thus being pure, and liberated from the madness of body, it is proper to believe that we shall then associate with others who are similarly pure, and shall through ourselves know everything genuine and sincere: and this perhaps is the truth itself; for it is by no means lawful that the pure should be touched by that which is impure. And such, O Simmias, in my opinion, ought to be the discourse and sentiments of all such as are lovers of learning in a proper manner. Or does it not seem so to you?

It does, Socrates, more so than anything.

If all this then, says Socrates, is true, my friend, much hope remains for him who arrives at that place to which I am now departing, that he shall there, if ever anywhere, sufficiently obtain that for the sake of which we take so much pains in the present life: so that the journey which is now assigned me will be accompanied with good hope; as will likewise be the case with any other man who thinks that he ought to prepare his danoëtic part in such a manner that it may become as it were pure.

Entirely so, says Simmias.

But does not purification consist in this, as we formerly asserted in our discourse: I mean in separating the soul from the body in the most eminent degree, and in accustoming it to call together and collect itself essentially on all sides from the body, and to dwell as much as possible, both now and hereafter, alone by itself, becoming by this means liberated from the body as from detaining bonds?

Entirely so, says he.

Is not death called a solution and separation of the soul from body?

Perfectly so, says he.

But those alone who philosophise rightly, as we have said, always and especially long for solution of the soul: and this is the meditation of philosophers, a solution and separation of the soul from the body; or do you not think so?

I do.

Would it not, therefore, as I said at first, be ridiculous for a man who has so prepared himself in the present life as to approach very near to death, to live indeed in the manner we have described, and yet, when death arrives, be afflicted? would this not be ridiculous?

How indeed should it not?

In reality, therefore, says he, O Simmias, those who philosophise rightly will mediate how to *die*; and *to be dead* will be to them of all men a thing the least terrible. But from hence consider as follows: for if they are on all sides enemies to the body, but desire to possess the soul subsisting by itself, would it not be very irrational for them to be terrified and troubled when death approaches, and to be unwilling to depart to that place, where when they have arrived they may hope to enjoy that which they were lovers of in the present life (but they were lovers of wisdom), and to be liberated from the association of that nature to which they were always inimical? Or do you think it possible, that many should be willing, of their own accord, to descend into Hades, allured by the hope of seeing and conversing with departed beautiful youths, wives and children whom they have loved; and that the true lover of wisdom, who has exceedingly nourished this hope, that he shall never possess wisdom as he ought anywhere but in Hades, should be afflicted when dying, and should not depart thither with readiness and delight? For it is necessary, my friend, to think in this manner of one who is a true philosopher; since such a one is very much of opinion that he shall never anywhere, but in that place, acquire the possession of wisdom with purity; and if this be the case, would it not be very irrational, as we just now said, for a man of this kind to be terrified at death?

Very much so, by Zeus, says he.

This then will be an argument sufficient to convince you, that he whom you behold to be afflicted, when about to die, is not a philosopher, but a lover of body; and this same person is a lover of riches and honors, either desiring the possession of one of these, or of both.

The case is entirely so, says he, as you represent it.

Does not then, O Simmias, that which is called fortitude eminently belong to philosophers?

Entirely so, says he.

Does not temperance also, which even the multitude thus denominate as a virtue, through which we are not agitated by desires, but regard them with moderation and contempt; does it not, I say, belong to those only who despise the body in the most eminent degree, and live in the exercise of philosophy?

It is necessary, says he.

For, if you are willing, says Socrates, to consider the fortitude and temperance of others, they will appear to you to be absurdities.

But how, Socrates?

You know, says he, that all others look upon death as a very great evil.

In the highest degree so, says he.

And those who are bold among these, sustain death when they do sustain it, through the dread of greater evils.

They do so.

All men, therefore, except philosophers, are bold through fearing and dread, though it is absurd that any one should be bold through fear or cowardice.

Entirely so.

But what, are not the moderate among these affected in the same manner? and are they not temperate by a certain intemperance? Though this is in a certain respect impossible, yet a passion similar to this happens to them with respect to this foolish temperance: for, fearing to be deprived of other pleasures which at the same time they desire, they abstain from the one being vanquished by others. And though they call intemperance a subjection to pleasures; yet at the same time it happens to them, that, being vanquished by certain pleasures, they control others; and this is similar to what I just now said, that after a certain manner they become temperate through intemperance.

It seems so, indeed.

But, O blessed Simmias, this is by no means the right road to virtue, to change pleasures for pleasures, pains for pains, fear for fear, and the greater for the lesser, like pieces of money: but that alone is the proper coin, I mean wisdom, for which all these ought to be changed. And indeed, for the sake of this, and with this everything must in reality be bought and sold, both fortitude and temperance, justice, and, in one word, true virtue, which subsists with wisdom, whether pleasures and pains, and everything else of this kind, are present or absent: but if these are separated from wisdom, and changed one with another, such virtue does not merit to be called even a shadowy description, but is in reality servile, and possesses nothing salutary and true. But that which is in reality true virtue is a purification from everything of this kind; and temperance and justice, fortitude, and thought itself, are each of them a certain purification. And those who instituted the Mysteries for us appear to have had a true and deep meaning when they signified formerly, in an obscure manner, *that whoever descended into Hades uninitiated, and without being a partaker of the Mysteries, should be plunged into mire; but that whoever arrived there, purified and initiated, should dwell with the gods.* For, as it is said by those who write about the Mysteries,

> The thyrsus-bearers numerous are seen,
> But few the Bacchuses have always been.

These few are, in my opinion, no other than those who philosophise rightly; and that I may be ranked in the number of these, I shall leave nothing unattempted, but exert myself in all possible ways. But whether or not my exertions have been properly directed, and whether I have accomplished anything, I think, if Divinity pleases, I shall clearly know very shortly when I arrive thither. And this, says he, Simmias and Cebes, is my apology, why upon leaving you, and the rulers of the present life, I ought not to be afflicted and indignant, since I am persuaded that I shall there meet with masters and companions not less good than such as are here. This indeed is incredible to many; but I am well content if my apology shall have more influence with you than with the judges of the Athenians.

When Socrates had thus spoken, Cebes, renewing the discourse, said, Other things, Socrates, appear to me to be well spoken; but what you have asserted about the soul will produce in men much incredulity, who think, when it is liberated from the body, that it is no longer anywhere, but that, on that very day in which a man dies, it is destroyed and perishes, and this immediately as it is freed from the body;[1] and, besides this, that on its departure it becomes dissipated like wind or smoke, makes its escape, and flies away, and is no longer anywhere: for if it remained anywhere essentially collected in itself, and liberated from those evils which you have now enumerated, there would be an abundant and fair hope, Socrates, that what you have asserted is true. But it will perhaps require no small persuasion and faith, in order to be persuaded that the soul remains, though the man dies, and that it possesses a certain power and thought.

You speak the truth, Cebes, says Socrates; but what shall we do? Are you willing that we should discourse about these particulars, whether it is likely that this should be the case with the soul, or not?

Indeed, says Cebes, I shall hear with great pleasure your opinion on this subject?

For I do not think, answered Socrates, that any one who should hear this discussion, even though he should be a comic poet, could say that I trifled, and discoursed about things not accommodated to my condition. If it is agreeable to you, therefore, and it is requisite to investi-

[1] The doctrine of annihilation.

gate these particulars, let us consider whether the souls of dead men survive in Hades, or not.

The assertion indeed, which we now call to mind, is an ancient one, I mean that souls departing from hence exist in Hades, and that they again return hither, and are generated from the dead.[1] And if the case is such, that living natures are again generated from the dead, can there be any other consequence than that our souls are there? for they could not be again generated if they had no subsistence; and this will be sufficient argument that these things are so, if it is really evident that the living can not be generated from anything else than the dead. But, if this is not the case, it will be necessary to adduce some other reason.

Entirely so, says Cebes.

You should not, therefore, says he, consider this assertion with respect to men alone, if you wish to learn with facility; but we should survey it as connected with all animals and plants, and in one word, with everything which is endued with generation. And not all things, therefore so generated, that they are produced no otherwise than contraries from contraries, I mean those which have any contrary? as the beautiful is contrary to the base, and the just to the unjust; and a thousand other particulars subsist in the same manner. We should consider, therefore, whether it is necessary, respecting everything which has a contrary, that this contrary should be generated from nothing else than that which is its contrary. As for instance, is it not necessary that, when anything becomes greater, it should become so from being before smaller?

[1] The doctrine of generation of life through death.

It is so, says he.

And is not the weaker generated from the stronger, and the swifter from the slower?

Entirely so.

But what if anything becomes worse, must it not become so from the better? and if more just, must it not be generated from the more unjust?

How should it not?

We have then, says he, sufficiently determined this, that everything is thus generated—viz., contraries from contraries.

Entirely so.

But what, is there anything among these which has a middle subsistence between both (since all contraries are two), so as to cause two generations from this to that, and from that again to this? for between the greater thing and the lesser thing there is an increasing and a diminution; and hence we say that the one is increased, but the other diminished.

It is so, says he.

And must not to be separated and mingled, to be cooled and heated, and everything in the same manner, though sometimes we do not distinguish the several particulars by names, must they not in reality be everywhere thus circumstanced, be generated from each other, and pass by generation into one another?

Entirely so, says he.

What then, says Socrates, is there anything contrary to the being alive, as sleeping is contrary to waking?

Entirely so, says he.

But what is this contrary?

To be dead.

Are not these, therefore, generated from each other, since they are contraries? and since they are two, are there not two processes of generation between them?

How should there not?

I will, therefore, says Socrates, tell you what one of these conjunctions is which I have just now spoken of, and what its generations are; do you tell me what the other is. But I say, that the one of these is to *sleep*, but the other *to awake;* and from sleeping awaking is generated, and from awaking sleeping; and the generations of these are on the one hand to be laid asleep, and on the other to be roused. Have I sufficiently explained this to you or not?

Perfectly so.

Do you, therefore, says he, inform me, in a similar manner, concerning life and death. Do you not say that *living* is the contrary of *to be dead?*

I do.

And that they are generated from each other?

Certainly.

What then is generated from that which is alive?

That which is dead, says he.

But what, says Socrates, is generated from *the dead?*

It is necessary to confess, says he, that this must be *the living*.

From the dead, therefore, says he, O Cebes, living things, and men who are alive, are generated.

It appears so, says he.

Our souls, therefore, says Socrates, subsist in Hades.

So it seems.

Is not, therefore, one of the processes of generation subsisting about these manifest? for *to die* is, I think, sufficiently clear; is it not?

Entirely so, says he.

What then shall we do? shall we not render back a contrary generation in its turn, but say that nature is defective and lame in this particular? Or is it necessary to assign a certain contrary process *to the being dead?*

Entirely so, says he.

But what is this?

To be restored back again to life.

But, says Socrates, if there is such a thing as to revive again, will not this reviving be a generation from the dead to the living?

Perfectly so.

This then is agreed upon by us, that the living are generated from the dead no less than the dead from the living: but, this being the case, it is a sufficient argument to prove that the souls of the dead must necessarily exist somewhere, from whence they may again be generated.

It appears to me, says he, Socrates, that this must necessarily follow from what has been admitted.

Take notice, then, says he, O Cebes! that we have not unjustly made these concessions, as it appears to me: for if other things, when generated, were not always restored in the place of others, revolving as it were in a circle, but generation subsisted according to a right line, proceeding from one thing alone into its opposite, without recurring again to the other, and making an inflection, you know. that all things would at length possess the same form, would be affected with the same passion, and would cease to be generated.

How do you say? says he.

It is by no means difficult, replies Socrates, to understand what I assert; but just as if there should be such a thing as falling asleep without recurring again to a state of waking, generated from a sleepy condition, you know that all things would at length exhibit the delusions of Endymion,[1] and nothing would be anything any more, because everything would suffer the same as happened to him—viz., would be laid asleep. And if all things went on being united, without ever being separated, the doctrine of Anaxagoras would soon be verified; for all things would be one confused mass. In the same manner, my dear Simmias, if all such things as participate of life should die, and after they are dead should abide in that lifeless form, and not revive again, would there not be a great necessity that all things should at length die, and that nothing should live? for if living beings are generated from other things, and living beings die, how can it be otherwise but that all things must be extinguished through being dead?

It appears to me, Socrates, says Cebes, that it cannot be otherwise; and in my opinion you perfectly speak the truth.

For to me, Cebes, says Socrates, it seems that nothing is so certain, and that we have not assented to this through deception; but that there is such a thing in reality as reviving again; that the living are generated from the dead; that the souls of the dead have a subsistence; and that the condition of the good after this life will be better than at present; but of the evil, worse.

But, says Cebes, interrupting him, according to that

---

[1] Endymion, the beautiful youth, with whom the goddess Diana fell in love. Zeus caused the youth to fall into an everlasting sleep, but allowed him to retain his beauty.

doctrine, Socrates, which you are frequently accustomed to employ (if it is true), that learning, with respect to us, is nothing else than reminiscence; according to this, it is necessary that we must have learned the things which we now call to mind in some former period of time. But this is impossible, unless our soul subsisted somewhere before it took up its residence in this human form; so that from hence the soul will appear to be a certain immortal nature.

But Cebes, says Simmias, interrupting him, recall into my memory what demonstrations there are of these particulars; for I do not very much remember them at present.

The truth of this, says Cebes, is evinced by one argument, and that a most beautiful one; that men, when interrogated, if they are but interrogated properly, will speak about everything correctly. At the same time, they could never do this unless science and right reason resided in their natures. And, in the second place, if any one leads them to diagrams,[1] or anything of this kind, he will in these most clearly discover that this is really the case.

But if you are not persuaded from this, Simmias, says Socrates, see if, from considering the subject in this manner, you will perceive as we do. For you do not understand how that which is called learning is reminiscence.

I do not disbelieve it, says Simmias; but I desire to be informed concerning this, which is the subject of our discourse, I mean reminiscence; and indeed, from what Cebes has endeavored to say, I almost now remember, and

---

[1] Diagrams—that is, geometrical figures. Cebes seems to mean that the obvious and necessary quality of geometrical truths implies some cognition of them prior to the experience of the present life. In point of fact it does more, it implies something prior to all experience.

am persuaded: but nevertheless I would at present hear how you attempt to support this opinion.

We defend it then, says Socrates, as follows: we confess without doubt, that if any one calls anything to mind, it is necessary that at some time or other he should have previously known this.

Entirely so, says he.

Shall we not confess this also, says Socrates, that when science is produced in us, after some particular manner, it is reminiscence? But I mean by a particular manner, thus: If any one, upon seeing or hearing anything, or apprehending it through the medium of any other sense, should not only know *it*, but should also think upon something else, of which there is not the same, but a different science, should we not justly say, that he recollects or remembers the particular, of which he receives a mental conception?

How do you mean?

Thus, says Socrates: In a certain respect the science of a man is different from that of a lyre.

How should it not?

Do you not, therefore, know that lovers when they see a lyre, or a vestment or anything else which the objects of their affection were accustomed to use, no sooner know the lyre, than they immediately receive in their intellectual part the form of the beloved person to whom the lyre belonged? But this is no other than reminiscence: just as any one, upon seeing Simmias, often recollects Cebes; and in a certain respect an infinite number of such particulars continually occur.[1]

An infinite number indeed, by Zeus, says Simmias.

[1] Association of ideas.

Is not then, says Socrates, something of this kind a certain reminiscence; and then especially so, when any one experiences this affection about things which, through time, and ceasing to consider them, he has now forgotten?

Entirely so, says Simmias.

But what, says Socrates, does it happen, that when any one sees a painted horse and a painted lyre, he calls to mind a man? and that when he beholds a picture of Simmias, he recollects Cebes?

Entirely so.

And will it not also happen, that on seeing a picture of Simmias he will recollect Simmias himself?

It certainly will happen so, says he.

Does it not therefore follow, that in all these instances reminiscence partly takes place from things similar, and partly from such as are dissimilar?

It does.

But when any one recollects anything from similars, must it not also happen to him, that he must know whether this similitude is deficient in any respect, as to likeness, from that particular of which he has the remembrance?

It is necessary, says he.

Consider then, says Socrates, if the following particulars are thus circumstanced. Do we say that there is such a thing as the Equal? I do not say one piece of wood to another, nor one stone to another, nor anything else of this kind; but do we say that the equal itself, which is something different from all these, is something or nothing?

We say it is something, by Zeus, Socrates, says Simmias, and that most confidently.

Have we also a scientific knowledge of that which is equal itself?

Entirely so, says he.

But from whence do we receive the science of it? Is it not from the particulars we have just now spoken of—viz., on seeing wood, stones or other things of this kind, which are equals, do we not form a conception of that equal which is different from these? But consider the affair in this manner: Do not equal stones and pieces of wood, although they remain the same, at one time appear equal, and at another not?

Entirely so.

But what, can *equals themselves* ever appear to you unequal? or can equality seem to be inequality?

By no means, Socrates.

These equals, therefore, are not the same with the equal itself.

By no means, Socrates, as it appears to me.

But from these equals, says he, which are different from the equal itself, you at the same time understand and receive the science of the *equal itself.*

You speak most true, says he.

Is it not, therefore, either similar to these or dissimilar?

Entirely so.

But indeed, says Socrates, this is of no consequence: for while, in consequence of seeing one thing, you understand another, from the view of this, whether it is dissimilar or similar, it is necessary that this conception of another thing should be reminiscence.

Entirely so.

But what will you determine concerning this? says

Socrates. Do we suffer anything of this kind respecting the equality in pieces of wood, and other such equals as we have just now spoken of? and do they appear to us to be equal in the same manner as the equal itself? and is something or nothing wanting, through which they are less equal than the equal itself?

There is much wanting, says he.

Must we not, therefore, confess, that when any one, on beholding some particular thing, understands that he wishes this, which I now behold, to be such as something else is, but that it is deficient, and falls short of its perfection; must we not confess that he who understands this, necessarily had a previous knowledge of that to which he asserts this to be similar, but in a defective degree?

It is necessary.

What then, do we feel something of this kind or not about equals and the equal itself?

Perfectly so.

It is necessary, therefore, that we must have previously known the *equal itself* before that time, in which, from first seeing equal things, we understood that we desired all these to be such as the *equal itself*, but that they had a defective subsistence.

It is so.

But this also we must confess, that we neither understood this, nor are able to understand it, by any other means than either through the sight, or the touch, or some other of the senses.

I speak in the same manner about all these. For they are the same, Socrates, with respect to that which your discourse wishes to evince.

From the senses then we come to understand that all

equals in sensible objects aspire after the *equal itself*, and are deficient from its perfection. Or how shall we say? In this manner: Before we begin to see, or hear, and to perceive other things, it necessarily follows, that we must in a certain respect have received the science of the *equal itself*, so as to know what it is, or else we could never refer the equals among sensibles to the *equal itself*, and be convinced that all these desire to become such as the *equal itself*, but fall short of its perfection.

This, Socrates, is necessary, from what has been previously said.

But do we not, as soon as we are born, see and hear, and possess the other senses?

Entirely so.

But we have said it is necessary that prior to these we should have received the science of the *equal itself*.

Certainly.

We must necessarily, therefore, as it appears, have received it before we were born.

It appears so.

If, therefore, receiving this before we were born, we were born possessing it; we both knew prior to our birth, and as soon as we were born, not only *the equal, the greater*, and *the lesser*, but everything of this kind: for our discourse at present is not more concerning *the equal* than *the beautiful, the good, the just*, and *the holy*, and in one word, about everything which we mark with the signature of *that which is*, both in our interrogations when we interrogate, and in our answers when we reply: so that it is necessary we should have received the science of all these before we were born.

All this is true.

And if, since we receive these sciences, we did not forget each of them, we should always be born knowing, and should always know them, through the whole course of our life: for to know is nothing else than this, to retain the science which we have received, and not to lose it. Or do we not call oblivion the loss of science?

Entirely so, says he, Socrates.

But if, receiving science before we were born, we lose it at the time of our birth, and afterwards, through exercising the senses about these particulars, receive back again those sciences which we once before possessed, will not that which we call learning be a recovery of our own proper science? and shall we not speak rightly when we call this a kind of reminiscence?

Entirely so.

For this appears to be possible, that when any one perceives anything, either by seeing or hearing, or employing any other sense, he may at the same time know something different from this, which he had forgotten, and to which this is similar, or to which it approaches, if it is dissimilar. So that, as I said, one of these two things must be the consequence: either that we were born knowing these, and possess a knowledge of all of them, through the whole of our life: or that we only remember what we are said to learn afterwards; and thus learning will be reminiscence.

The case is perfectly so, Socrates.

Which, therefore, will you choose, Simmias: that we are born knowing, or that we afterwards remember the particulars of which we formerly received the science?

At present, Socrates, I have no choice.

But what will be your choice in the following instance,

and what will be your opinion about it? Can a man, who possesses science, render a reason concerning the objects of his knowledge, or not?

There is a great necessity, says he, Socrates, that he should.

And does it also appear to you, that all men can render a reason of the particulars concerning which we have just now spoken?

I wish they could, says Simmias; but I am much more afraid that to-morrow at this hour there will no longer be any one here capable of doing this.

You do not therefore think, Simmias, that all men know these particulars?

By no means.

They remember, therefore, the things which they have once learned.

It is necessary.

But when did our souls receive this science? for they did not receive them from those from whom we are born men.

Certainly not.

Before this period, therefore.

Certainly.

Our souls, therefore, Simmias, had a subsistence before they were in a human form, separate from bodies, and possessed intelligence.

Unless, Socrates, we received these sciences while we were making our entrance into the present life; for that space of time is yet left for us.

Let it be so, my friend. But in what other time did we lose these? for we were not born possessing them, as we have just now acknowledged. Did we lose them at the very time in which we received them? Or can you mention any other time?

By no means, Socrates: but I did not see that I spoke nothing to the purpose.

Will then the case remain thus for us, Simmias? for if those things have a subsistence which we perpetually proclaim—viz., a certain something beautiful and good, and every such essence; and if we refer to this all sensible objects, as finding it to have a prior subsistence, and to be ours, and assimulate these to it, as images to their exemplar; it is necessary that, as these essences have a subsistence, so likewise that our soul should have subsisted before we were born: but if these are not, this discourse will have been undertaken in vain. Is it not so? and is there not an equal necessity, both that these should have a subsistence, and that our souls should have had a being before we were born, and that the one cannot be without the other?

The same necessity, Socrates, says Simmias, appears to me to take place in a most transcendent manner; and the discourse flies to a beautiful circumstance, I mean the conjoined subsistence of our soul before we were born, and of that essence which you now speak of. For I possess nothing which is so clear to me as this, that all such things as the beautiful and the good subsist, in the most eminent degree, together with everything else which you mention; and, with respect to myself, it is sufficiently demonstrated.

But how does it appear to Cebes? says Socrates: for it is necessary that Cebes also should be persuaded.

In my opinion he is sufficiently so, says Simmias, although he is the most resolute of all men in not assenting to what is said. Yet I think he he is sufficiently persuaded that our soul had a subsistence before we were born. But whether or not the soul remains after death, does not appear to me, Socrates, says he, to be yet demonstrated; but that doubt of the multitude, which Cebes mentioned, still presses hard upon me, whether, when a man dies, the soul is not dissipated, and this is the end of its existence. For what hinders but that it may be born, and may have had a subsistence elsewhere, and this before it came into a human body; and yet, after it departs, and is liberated from this body, may then die and be corrupted?

You speak well, Simmias, says Cebes; for it appears that the half only of what was necessary has been demonstrated, I mean that our soul subsisted before we were born; but it is necessary that you should demonstrate, besides this, that it no less subsists after we are dead, than it did before we were born, in order that the demonstration may be complete.

This, Simmias and Cebes, says Socrates, is even now demonstrated, if you are only willing to connect into one and the same the present discourse, and that which we before assented to; I mean that every vital nature is generated from that which is dead. For if the soul had a prior subsistence, and it is necessary when it proceeds into the present life, and is generated man, that it should be generated from nothing else than death, and to be dead; how is it not necessary that it should also subsist after death, since it is requisite that it should be generated again? Its existence, thereafter, after death, is even now, as I said, demonstrated. But you and Simmias would gladly, it appears, search into the subject still further. You are afraid, like boys, lest on the soul's departure from the body the winds should tear it in pieces, and widely disperse it,—especially if any one should die during a stormy blast, and not when the heavens are serene!

Upon this Cebes laughing, Endeavor, says he, O Socrates, to persuade us of the contrary, as if we were afraid, or rather as if not we were afraid, but, perhaps, some boy among us,[1] by whom circumstances of this kind may be dreaded: him, therefore, we should endeavor to persuade not to be terrified at death, as if it were some dreadful spectre.

But it is necessary, says Socrates, to charm him every day till he becomes well.

But from whence, says he, O Socrates, can a man acquire skill in such enchantment, since you are about to leave us?

Greece, says he, Cebes, is very spacious, in some part of which good men may be found: and there are many barbarian nations, all which must be wandered over, inquiring after an enchanter of this kind, without sparing either riches or labor, as there is nothing for which wealth can be more seasonably bestowed. But it is necessary that you should inquire among yourselves; for perhaps you will not easily find any one who is more able to accomplish this than yourselves.

Let these things be so, says Cebes: but, if you please, let us return from whence we made this digression.

It will be agreeable to me, says Socrates: for how should it not be so?

You speak well, says Cebes.

Some such thing, therefore, says Socrates, we ought to

[1] Some boyish spirit in us.

inquire of ourselves—viz., what is naturally affected by dissolution; and respecting what we ought to fear, lest this should take place; and to whom a fear of this kind is proper; and after this, we should consider whether it is soul or not; and, as the result of these speculations, should either be confident or fearful concerning our soul.

You speak true, says he.

Is it not, therefore, natural to that which is collected together, and a composite, that it should be dissolved so far as it is a composite; and that, if there is anything without composition, to this alone, if to any other, it belongs not to suffer affections of this kind?

This, says Cebes, appears to me to be the case.

But does it not follow, that things which always subsist according to the same, and in a similar manner, are in the most eminent degree incomposites; but that such things as subsist differently at different times, and never according to the same, are composites?

To me it appears so.

Let us return, therefore, says he, to the particulars of our former discourse: Whether is *essence itself* (which both in our inquiries and answers we established as having a being) that which always subsists similarly, and according to the same, or that which subsists differently at different times? And does *the equal itself*, *the beautiful itself*, and everything which truly is, ever receive any kind of mutation? Or does not everything which always truly is, and has a uniform subsistence, essentially abide in a similar manner according to the same, and never in any respect receive any mutation?

It is necessary, Socrates, says Cebes, that it should subsist similarly, and according to the same.

But what shall we say concerning many beautiful things, such as men, horses, garments or other things of this kind, which are either equal or beautiful; and of all such as are synonymous to these? Do these also subsist according to the same, or rather are they not entirely contrary to those, so that they neither subsist similarly according to the same, either with respect to themselves or to one another, or, in one word, in any manner whatever?

These, says Cebes, never subsist in a similar condition.

These, therefore, may be touched, may be seen and perceived by the other senses; but those natures which always subsist according to the same, cannot be apprehended by any other means than the discursive energy of the intellectual power. But things of this kind are invisible, and cannot be seen.

You speak most truly, said Cebes.

Are you willing, therefore, says he, that we should establish two species of beings, the one visible, and the other invisible.

Let us establish them, says he.

And that the invisible subsists always according to the same, but the visible never according to the same.

And this also, says he, we will establish.

Come then, says Socrates, is there anything else belonging to us, than on the one hand body, and on the other soul?

Nothing else, says he.

To which species, therefore, shall we say the body is more similar and allied?

It is manifest to every one, says he, that it is allied to the visible species.

But what shall we say of the soul? Is it visible, or invisible?

It is certainly not visible to men, Socrates, says he.

But we speak of things which are visible or not so, with respect to the nature of men. Or do you think we speak of things visible to any other nature?

Of those which regard the nature of men.

What then shall we say respecting the soul, that it is visible, or cannot be seen?

That it cannot be seen.

The soul, therefore, is more similar to the invisible species than the body, but the body is more similar to the visible.

It is perfectly necessary it should be so, Socrates.

And have we not also formerly asserted this, that the soul, when it employs the body in the speculation of anything, either through sight, or hearing, or some other sense (for to speculate through sense is to speculate through body), then, indeed, it is drawn by the body to things which never subsist according to the same, wanders and is agitated, and becomes giddy like one intoxicated, through passing into contact with things of this kind?

Entirely so.

But when it speculates anything itself by itself, then it departs to that which is pure, eternal and immortal, and which possesses a sameness of subsistence: and, as being allied to such a nature, it perpetually becomes united with it, when it subsists alone by itself, and as often as it may: and then, too, it rests from its wanderings, and is ever the same being concerned and united with things that are ever the same; and this passion of the soul is denominated wisdom.

You speak, says he, Socrates, in every respect beautifully and true.

To which species, therefore, of things, formerly and now spoken of, does the soul appear to you to be more similar and allied?

It appears to me, Socrates, says he, that every one, and even the most indocile, must admit, in consequence of this method of reasoning, that the soul is both totally and universally more similar to that which subsists perpetually the same, than to that which does not so.

But to which is the body most similar?

To the other species.

But consider also as follows: that, since soul and body subsist together, nature commands that the one should be subservient and obey, but that the other should rule and possess dominion. And in consequence of this, which again of these appear to you to be similar to a divine nature, and which to the mortal nature? Or does it not appear to you that the divine nature is essentially adapted to govern and rule, but the mortal to be governed and be subservient?

To me it does so.

To which, therefore, is the soul similar?

It is manifest, Socrates, that the soul is similar to the divine, but the body to the mortal nature.

But consider, says he, Cebes, whether, from all that has been said, these conclusions will result to us, that the soul is most similar to the divine, immortal, intelligible, uniform and indissoluble nature, and which always subsists similarly according to the same; but that the body is most similar to the nature which is human, mortal, void of intellect, multiform, dissoluble and which never subsists according to the same. Can we, my dear Cebes, produce any arguments to show that this is not the case?

We cannot.

What then? in consequence of all this, must it not be the property of the body, to be swiftly dissolved; but of the soul, on the contrary, to be entirely indissoluble, or something bordering on such a state?

How should it not?

Do you conceive, therefore, says he, that when a man dies, the visible part of him, or the body, which is situated in a visible region (and which we call a dead body subject to dissolution, ruin and dissipation), does not immediately suffer any of these affections, but remains for a considerable space of time; and if any one dies possessing a graceful body, that it very much retains its elegant form?[1] for, when the body is bound and buried according to the manner in which the Egyptians bury their dead, it remains almost entire for an incredible space of time; and though some parts of the body may become rotten, yet the bones and nerves, and everything of this kind, are preserved as one may say immortal. Is it not so?

Certainly.

Can the soul, therefore, which is invisible, and which departs into another place of this kind, a place noble, pure and invisible, viz., into Hades,[2] to a beneficent and prudent God (at which place, if Divinity is willing, my soul will shortly arrive); can the soul, I say, since it is naturally of this kind, be immediately dissipated and perish on its being liberated from the body, as is asserted by the many? This is certainly, my dear Cebes and Sim-

---

[1] At a time of life when the body is in full vigor.
[2] Hades, ἀ-ιδής, the invisible.

mias, far from being the case. But this will much more abundantly take place, if it is liberated in a pure condition, attracting to itself nothing of the body, as not having willingly communicated with it in the present life, but fled from it and collected itself into itself; an employment of this kind having been the subject of its perpetual meditation. But this is nothing else than to philosophise rightly, and to meditate with facility, how *to be dead in reality*. Or will this not be a meditation of death?

Entirely so.

Will not the soul, therefore, when in this condition, depart to that which is similar to itself, a divine nature, and which is likewise immortal and wise? and when it arrives thither, will it not become happy, being liberated from wandering and ignorance, terror and insane love, and from all other evils belonging to the human nature; and so, as it is said of the initiated, will in reality pass the rest of its time in the society of the gods? Shall we speak in this manner, Cebes, or otherwise?

In this manner, by Zeus, says Cebes.

But I think that if the soul departs polluted and impure from the body, as having always been its associate, attending upon and loving the body, and becoming enchanted by it, through its desires and pleasures, in such a manner as to think that nothing really is, except what is corporeal, which can be touched and seen, eaten and drunk, and at the same time is accustomed to hate, dread and avoid that which is dark and invisible to the eye of sense, which is intelligible and apprehended by philosophy; do you think that a soul thus affected can be liberated from the body, so as to subsist sincerely by itself?

By no means, says he.

But I think that it will be contaminated by a corporeal nature, to which its converse and familiarity with the body, through perpetual association and abundant meditation, have rendered it similar and allied.

Entirely so.

But it is proper, my dear Cebes, to think that such a nature is ponderous and heavy, terrestrial and visible; and that a soul of this kind, through being connected with such a nature, is rendered heavy, and drawn down again into the visible region from its dread of that which is invisible and Hades, and, as it is said, wanders about monuments and tombs; about which indeed certain shadowy phantoms of souls appear, being the images produced by such souls as have not been purely liberated from the body, but which participate of the visible nature; and on this account they become visible.

It is very reasonable to suppose so, Socrates.

It is reasonable indeed, Cebes: and likewise that these are not the souls of the worthy, but of the depraved, who are compelled to wander about such places; by these means suffering the punishment of their former conduct, which was evil; and they are compelled thus to wander till, through the desire of a corporeal nature, which attends them, they are again bound to a body. They are bound, however, as it is proper they should be, to such manners as they have exercised in the present life.

But what do you say these manners are, Socrates?

As, for example, that such as are addicted to gluttony, arrogant injuries, and drinking, and have no pruduce nor reverence, shall enter into the tribes of asses and brutes of this kind. Or do you not think it proper that they should?

You speak in a manner perfectly becoming.

But shall we not say, that such as held in the highest estimation injustice, tyranny and rapine shall enter into the tribes of wolves, hawks and kites? Or where else can we say such souls depart?

Into tribes of this kind, certainly, says Cebes.

It will, therefore, be manifest concerning the rest into what nature each departs, according to the similitudes of manners which they have exercised.

It is manifest, says he; for how should it not be so?

Are not, therefore, says he, those among these the most happy, and such as depart into the best place, who have made popular and social virtue their study, which they call indeed temperance and justice, and which is produced from custom and exercise, without philosophy and intellect?

But how are these the most happy?

Because it is fit that these should again migrate into a social and mild tribe of this kind; such as bees, wasps or ants, or into the same human tribe again, and become temperate and orderly men.

It is fit.

But it is not lawful for any to pass into the genus of gods, except such as, through a love of learning, have philosophised, and departed from hence perfectly pure. And for the sake of this, my dear Simmias and Cebes, those who have philosophised rightly abstain from all desires belonging to the body, and strenuously presevere in this abstinence, without giving themselves up to their dominion; nor is it because they dread the ruin of their families and poverty, like the multitude of the lovers of wealth; nor yet because they are afraid of ignominy and the infamy of improbity, like those who are lovers of dominion and honors, that they abstain from these desires.

For it would not, Socrates, become them so to do, says Cebes.

It would not, by Zeus, says he. Hence those, O Cebes! who take care of their soul, and do not live in a state of subserviency to their bodies, bidding farewell to all such characters as we have mentioned above, do not proceed in the same path with these during the journey of life, because such characters are ignorant how they should direct their course; but considering that they ought not to act contrary to philosophy, and to its solution and purification, they give themselves up to its direction, and follow wherever it leads.

In what manner, Socrates?

I will tell you.

The lovers of learning well know, that when philosophy receives their soul into her protection (and when she does so, she finds it vehemently bound and agglutinated to the body, and compelled to speculate things through this, as through a place of confinement, instead of beholding herself through herself; and besides this, rolled in every kind of ignorance : philosophy likewise beholds the dire nature of the confinement, and it arises through desire; so that he who is bound in an eminent degree assists in binding himself); the lovers of learning therefore, I say, know that philosophy, receiving their soul in this condition, endeavors gently to exhort it, and dissolve its bonds; and this she attempts to accomplish, by showing that the inspection of things through the eyes is full of deception, and that this is likewise the case with perception through the ears and the other senses. Philosophy too persuades the soul to depart from all these fallacious informations, and to employ them no further than necessity requires; and exhorts her to call together and collect herself into one. And besides this, to believe in no other than herself, with respect to what she understands, herself subsisting by herself, of that which has likewise a real subsistence by itself; and not to consider that as having a true being which she speculates through others, and which has its subsistence in others.[1] And lastly, that a thing of this kind is sensible and visible; but that what she herself perceives is intelligible and invisible. The soul of a true philosopher, therefore, thinking that he ought not to oppose this deliverance, abstains as much as possible from pleasures and desires, griefs and fears, considering that when any one is vehemently delighted or terrified, afflicted or desirous, he does not suffer any such mighty evil from these as some one may perhaps conceive, I mean such as disease and a consumption of wealth, through indulging his desires; but that he suffers that which is the greatest, and the extremity of all evils, and this without apprehending that he does so.

But what is this evil, Socrates, says Cebes.

That the soul of every man is compelled at the same time to be either vehemently delighted or afflicted about some particular thing, and to consider that about which it is thus affected, as having a most evident and true subsistence, though this is by no means the case; and that these are most especially visible objects. Is it not so?

Entirely.

---

[1] The soul alone can perceive the truth, but the senses, being different, receive and convey different impressions of the same thing; the eye does not receive the same impression of an object as the ear.

In this passion, therefore, is not the soul in the highest degree bound to the body?

In what manner?

Because every pleasure and pain, as if armed with a nail, fasten and rivet the soul to the body, cause it to become corporeal, and fill it with an opinion, that whatever the body asserts is true. For, in consequence of the soul forming the same opinions with the body, and being delighted with the same objects, it appears to me that it is compelled to possess similar manners, and to be similarly nourished, and to become so affected, that it can never pass into Hades in a pure condition; but always departs full of a corporeal nature; and thus swiftly falls into another body, and becoming as it were sown, takes root and grows there; and lastly, that thus it comes to have no share in communion with that which is divine, pure and unchangeable.

You speak most true, Socrates, says Cebes.

For the sake of these things, therefore, O Cebes! those who are justly lovers of learning are well-conducted and courageous, and not for the sake of such as the multitude assert. Or do you think it is?

By no means; for it cannot be.

But the soul of a philosopher reasons in this manner; and does not think that philosophy ought to free him from the body, but that when he is freed he may give himself up to pleasures and pains, by which he will again be bound to the body, and will undertake a work which it is impossible to finish, reweaving, as it were, the web of Penelope. But procuring tranquillity with respect to these, and following the guidance of the reasoning power, and being always conversant with this, contemplating at the same time that which is true, divine, and not the subject of opinion, and being likewise nourished by such an object of contemplation, he will think that he ought to live in this manner while he lives, and that when he dies he shall depart to that which is akin to him—such as we have spoken of—being liberated from the maladies of the human nature. But from a nutriment of this kind the soul has no occasion to fear (while it makes these, O Simmias and Cebes! its study), lest, in its liberation from the body, it should be rent asunder, and, being blown about and dissipated by the winds, should vanish, and no longer have anywhere a subsistence.

When Socrates had thus spoken, a long silence ensued; and Socrates seemed to revolve with himself what had been said; as likewise did the greatest part of us: but Cebes and Simmias discoursed a little with each other. And Socrates at length looking upon them, What, says he, do our assertions appear to you to have been not sufficiently demonstrated? for many doubts and suspicions yet remain, if any one undertakes to investigate them sufficiently. If, therefore, you are considering something else among yourselves, I have nothing to say; but if you are doubting about those particulars which we have just now made the subject of our discourse, do not be remiss in speaking about and running over what has been said, if it appears to you in any respect that we might have spoken better; and receive me again as your associate, if you think that you can be any ways benefited by my assistance.

Upon this Simmias said, Indeed, Socrates, I will tell you the truth: for some time since each of us being agitated with doubts, we impelled and exhorted one another to interrogate you, through our desire of hearing them solved; but we were afraid of causing a debate, lest it should be disagreeable to you in your present circumstances. But Socrates, upon hearing this, gently laughed, and said, This is strange, indeed, Simmias; for I shall with difficulty be able to persuade other men that I do not consider the present fortune as a calamity, since I am not able to persuade even you; but you are afraid lest I should be more morose now than I was prior to the present event. And, as it seems, I appear to you to be more despicable than swans with respect to divination, who, when they perceive that it is necessary for them to die, sing not only as usual, but then more than ever; rejoicing that they are about to depart to that deity in whose service they are engaged. But men, because they themselves are afraid of death, falsely accuse the swans, and assert that, in consequence of their being afflicted at death, their song is the result of grief. Nor do they consider that no bird sings when it is hungry, or cold or is afflicted with any other malady; neither the nightingale, nor the swallow nor the lapwing, all which they say sing lamenting through distress. But neither do these birds, as it appears to me, sing through sorrow, nor yet the swans; but yet in my opinion these last are prophetic, as belonging to Apollo; and in consequence of foreseeing the good which Hades contains, they sing and rejoice at that period more remarkably than at any preceding time. But I consider myself as a fellow-servant of the swans, and sacred to the same Divinity. I possess a divining power from our common master no less than they; nor shall I be more afflicted than the swan in being liberated from the present life. Hence it is proper that you should both speak and inquire about whatever you please, as long as the eleven magistrates will permit.

If you are willing I will relate to you what happened to me; and afterwards, if anything which I shall say shall appear to you useful, employ it.

But I am most assuredly willing, says Cebes.

Hear then my narration: When I was a young man, Cebes, I was in a wonderful manner desirous of that wisdom which they call a history of nature: for it appeared to me to be a very superb affair to know the causes of each particular, on what account each is generated, why it perishes, and why it exists. And I often tossed myself as it were upwards and downwards; considering, in the first place, whether after that which is hot and cold has received a certain rottenness, as some say, then animals are nourished; and whether the blood is that through which we have intelligence, or air or fire; or whether none of these, but the brain, is that which affords the senses of seeing, hearing and smelling; so that memory and opinion are generated from these, and that from memory and opinion obtaining fixity, Science is accordingly produced? And again considering the corruptions of these, and the changes with which the heavens and the earth are affected, I at length appeared to myself so unskillful in the speculation of these, as to receive no advantage from my inquiries. But I will give you a sufficient proof of the truth of this: for I then became so very blind, with respect to things which I knew before with great clearness (as it appeared both to myself and others) through this speculation, as to want instruction both in many particulars, which I thought I had known before, and in this, too, how a man is increased. For I thought it was evident to every one that this took place through eating and drinking; for when, from the ailment, flesh accedes to flesh, bone to bone, and everywhere kindred to kindred parts, then the bulk which was small becomes afterward great; and thus a little man becomes a large one. Such was then my opinion; does it appear to you a becoming one?

To me, indeed, it does, says Cebes.

But still further, consider as follows: for I thought that I seemed to myself sufficiently right in my opinion, when, on seeing a tall man standing by a short one, I judged that he was taller by the head; and in like manner one horse than another: and still more evident than these, ten things appeared to me to be more than eight, because two is added to them, and that a bicubital is greater than a cubital magnitude, through its surpassing it by the half.

But now, says Cebes, what appears to you respecting these?

By Zeus, says he, I am so far from thinking that I know the cause of these, that I cannot even persuade myself, when any one person adds one to one, that then the one to which the addition was made becomes two, or that the added one and that to which it is added, become two, through the addition of the one to the other. For I should wonder, since each of these, when separate from one another, was one, and not then two; if, after they have approached nearer to each other, this should be the cause of their becoming two—viz., the association through which they are placed nearer to each other. Nor yet, if any person should divide one, am I able to persuade myself that this division is the cause of its becoming two. For that former cause of two being produced is contrary to this. For then this took place, because they were collected near to each other, and the one was applied to the other; but now, because the one is removed and separated from the other. Nor do I any longer persuade myself, that I know why one is produced; nor, in one word, why anything else is either generated or destroyed, or is, according to this method of proceeding: but, in order to obtain this knowledge, I mix in, in some random fashion of my own, a new method, by no means admitting this which I have mentioned.

But having once heard a person reading from a certain book, composed, as he said, by Anaxagoras—when he came to that part in which he says that intellect orders and is the cause of all things, I was delighted with this cause, and thought that, in a certain respect, it was an excellent thing for intellect to be the cause of all; and I considered that, if this was the case, disposing intellect would adorn all things, and place everything in that situation in which it would subsist in the best manner. If any one, therefore, should be willing to discover the cause through which everything is generated, or destroyed, or is, he ought to discover how it may subsist in the best manner, or suffer or perform anything else. In consequence of this, therefore, it is proper that a man should consider nothing else, either about himself or about others, except that which is the most excellent and the best: but it is necessary that he who knows this should also know that which is subordinate, since there is one and the same science of both. But thus reasoning with myself, I rejoiced, thinking that I had found a preceptor in Anaxagoras, who would instruct me in the causes of things agreeably to my own conceptions; and that he would inform me, in the first place, whether the earth is flat or round ; and afterwards explain the cause and necessity of its being so, adducing for this purpose that which is better, and showing that it is better for the earth to exist in this manner. And if he should say it is situated in the middle, that he would, besides this, show that it is better for it to be in the middle : and if he should render all this apparent to me, I was so disposed as not to require any other species of cause. I had likewise prepared myself in a similar manner for any inquiry respecting the sun and moon, and the other stars, their velocities and revolutions about each other, and all their other properties ; so as to be able to know why it is better for each to operate in a certain manner, and to suffer that which it suffers. For I by no means thought, after he had said that all these were orderly disposed by intellect, he would introduce any other cause of their subsistence, except that which shows that it is best for them to exist as they do. Hence I thought that in assigning the cause common to each particular, and to all things, he would explain that which is best for each, and is the common good of all. And indeed I would not have exchanged these hopes for a mighty gain ! but having obtained his books with prodigious eagerness, I read them with great celerity, that I might with great celerity know that which is the best, and that which is bad.

From this admirable hope, however, my friend, I was forced away, when, in the course of my reading, I saw him make no use of intellect, nor employ certain causes, for the purpose of orderly disposing particulars, but assign air, æther and water, and many other things equally absurd, as the causes of things. And he appeared to me to be affected in a manner similar to him who should assert, that all the actions of Socrates are produced by intellect; and afterwards, endeavoring to relate the causes of each particular action, should say, that, in the first place, I now sit here because my body is composed from bones and nerves, and that the bones are solid, and are separated by intervals from each other; but that the nerves, which are of a nature capable of intension and relaxation, cover the bones, together with the flesh and skin by which they are contained. The bones, therefore, being suspended from their joints, the nerves, by straining and relaxing them, enable me to bend my limbs as at present; and through this cause I here sit in an inflected position—and again, should assign other suchlike causes of my conversation with you—viz., voice, and air and hearing, and a thousand other such particulars, neglecting to adduce the true cause, that since it appeared to the Athenians better to condemn me, on this account, it also appeared to me to be better and more just to sit here, and, thus abiding, sustain the punishment which they have ordained me. For otherwise, by the Dog, as it appears to me, these nerves and bones would have been carried long ago either into Megara or Bœotia, through an opinion of that which is best, if I had not thought it more just and becoming to sustain the punishment ordered by my country, whatever it might be, than to withdraw myself and run away. But to call things of this kind causes is extremely absurd. Indeed, if any one should say that without possessing such things as bones and nerves, and other particulars which belong to me, I could not do the things I think right, he would speak the truth: but to assert that I act as I do at present through these, and that with these things intellect is concerned and not with the choice of what is best, would be an assertion full of extreme negligence and sloth. Not to be able to distinguish between the true cause of a thing and that without which the cause would not be a cause——! And this indeed appears to me to be the case with the multitude of mankind, who, handling things as it were in darkness, call them by names foreign from the truth, and thus denominate things causes which are not so. Hence, one placing round the earth a certain vortex, produced by the celestial motion, renders by this means the earth fixed in the center; but another places air under it, as if it was a basis to a broad trough. But they neither investigate that power through which things are now disposed in the best manner possible, nor do they think that it is endued with any divine strength: but they fancy they have found a certain Atlas, more strong and immortal than such a strength, and far more sustaining all things; and they think that the good and the becoming do not in reality connect and sustain anything. With respect to myself, indeed, I would most willingly become the disciple of any one: so that I might perceive in what manner a cause of this kind subsists. But since I am deprived of this advantage, and have neither been able to discover it myself, nor to learn it from another, are you willing, Cebes, that I should show you the manner in which, for the lack of better, I made inquiry into causes?

I am, says he, abundantly willing.

It appeared to me therefore, says Socrates, afterwards, when I had failed in my investigations of existence, that I ought to take care lest I should be affected in the same manner as those are who attentively behold the sun in an eclipse: for some would be deprived of their sight, unless they beheld its image in water, or in a similar medium. And something of this kind I perceived with respect to myself, and was afraid lest my soul should be perfectly blinded through beholding things with my eyes, and through endeavoring to apprehend them by means of the several senses. Hence I considered that I ought to fly to Reason, and in that survey the truth of things. Perhaps, indeed, this similitude of mine may not in a certain respect be proper: for I do not entirely admit that he who contemplates things in Reason, surveys them in images, more than he who contemplates them in external effects. This method, however, I have adopted; and always establishing that reason as an hypothesis, which I judge to be the most valid, whatever appears to me to be consonant to this, I fix upon as true, both concerning the cause of things and everything else; but such as are not consonant I consider as not true. But I wish to explain to you what I say in a clearer manner: for I think that you do not at present understand me.

Not very much, by Zeus, says Cebes.

However, says he, I now assert nothing new, but what I have always asserted at other times, and in the preceding disputation. For I shall now attempt to demonstrate to you that species of cause which I have been discoursing about, and shall return again to those particulars which are so much discussed; beginning from these, and laying down as an hypothesis, that there is a certain Beauty, itself subsisting by itself; and a certain Goodness and Greatness, and so of all the rest; which if you permit me to do, and allow that such things have a subsistence, I hope that I shall be able from these to demonstrate this cause to you, and discover that the soul is immortal.

But, says Cebes, in consequence of having granted you this already, you cannot be hindered from drawing such a conclusion.

But consider, says he, the things consequent on these, and see whether you will then likewise agree with me. For it appears to me, that if there be anything else beautiful, besides the Beautiful itself, it cannot be beautiful on any other account than because it participates of the Beautiful itself; and I should speak in the same manner of all things. Do you admit such a cause?

I admit it, says he.

I do not, therefore, says Socrates, any longer perceive, nor am I able to understand, those other ingenious causes; but if any one tells me why a certain thing is beautiful, and assigns as a reason, either its possessing a florid color, or figure, or something else of this kind, I bid farewell to all that, for it only confuses me; but this I retain with myself, simply, uncritically and perhaps foolishly, that nothing else causes it to be beautiful, than either the presence, or communion, or in whatever manner the operations may take place, of the Beautiful itself. For I cannot yet affirm how this takes place; but only this, that all beautiful things become such through the beautiful itself. For it appears to me most safe thus to answer both myself and others; and adhering to this, I think that I can never fall, but that I shall be secure in answering, that all beautiful things are beautiful through the Beautiful itself. Does it not also appear so to you?

It does.

And that great things, therefore, are great, and things

greater, greater through Magnitude itself; and things lesser, lesser through Smallness itself?

Certainly.

Neither, therefore, would you assent, if it should be said that some one is larger than another by the head, and that he who is lesser is lesser by the very same thing, *i.e.*, the head: but you would testify that you said nothing else than that, with respect to everything great, one thing is greater than another by nothing else than Magnitude, and that through this it is greater, *i.e.*, through Magnitude; and that the lesser is lesser through nothing else than Smallness, and that through this it is lesser, *i.e.*, through Smallness. For you would be afraid, I think, lest, if you should say that any one is greater and lesser by the head, you should contradict yourself: first, in asserting that the greater is greater, and the lesser lesser, by the very same thing; and afterwards that the greater by the head; which is a small thing; and that it is monstrous to suppose, that anything which is great can become so through something which is small. Would you not be afraid of all this?

Indeed I should, says Cebes, laughing.

Would you not also, says he, be afraid to say that ten things are more than eight by two, and that through this cause ten transcends eight, and not by Multitude and through Magnitude? And in like manner, that a thing which is two cubits in length is greater than that which is but one cubit, by the half, and not by Magnitude? for the dread is indeed the same.

Entirely so, says he.

But what? one being added to one, will the addition be the cause of their becoming two? or if one is divided, and two produced, would you not be afraid to assign division as the cause? Indeed you would cry with a loud voice, that you know no other way by which anything subsists, than by participating the proper essence of everything which it participates; and that in these you can assign no other cause of their becoming two, than the participation of the Duad; and that it is proper all such things as are about to become two, should participate of this, and of Unity, whatever is about to become one. But you would bid farewell to these divisions and additions, and other subtilties of this kind, and would leave them to be employed in answering, by those who are wiser than yourself. And fearing, as it is said, your own shadow, and your own unskillfulness, you would adhere to this safe hypothesis, and answer in the manner I have described. But if any one should attack this hypothesis, you would refrain from answering him till you had considered the consequences resulting from thence, and whether they were consonant or dissonant to one another. But when it is necessary for you to assign a reason for your belief in this hypothesis, you will assign it in a similar manner, laying down again another hypothesis, which shall appear to be the best of higher hypotheses, and so on, till you arrive at something sufficient. At the same time you will by no means confound things by mingling them together, after the manner of the contentious, when you discourse concerning the principle and the consequences arising from thence, if you are willing to discover anything of true being, For by such as these, perhaps, no attention is paid to this. For these, through their wisdom, are able to be quite content with the confusion they make. But you, if you rank among the philosophers, will act, I think, in the manner I have described.

Both Simmias and Cebes said, You speak most truly.

Echec. By Zeus, Phædo, they assented with great propriety : for he appears to me to have asserted this in a manner wonderfully clear ; and this even to one endued with the smallest degree of intellect.

Phæd. And so, indeed, Echecrates, it appeared in every respect to all who were present.

Echec. And well it might : for it appears so to us, now we hear it, who were not present. But what was the discourse after this?

If I remember right, after they had granted all this, and had confessed that each of the several species was something, and that others participating of these received the same denomination, he afterwards interrogated them as follows : If then you allow that these things are so, when you say that Simmias is larger than Socrates, but less than Phædo, do you not then assert that both Magnitude and Parvitude are inherent in Simmias?

I do.

And yet, says he, you must confess that this circumstance of Simmias surpassing Socrates, does not truly subsist in the manner which the words seem to imply. For Simmias is not naturally adapted to surpass Socrates, so far as he is Simmias, but by the magnitude which he possesses : nor, again, does he surpass Socrates so far as Socrates is Socrates, but because Socrates possesses parvitude with respect to his magnitude.

True.

Nor again is Simmias surpassed by Phædo, because Phædo is Phædo, but because Phædo possesses magnitude with respect to the parvitude of Simmias.

It is so.

Simmias, therefore, is allotted the appellation of both small and great, being situated in the middle of both; exhibiting his smallness to be surpassed by the greatness of the one, and his greatness to the other's smallness, which it surpasses. And at the same time, gently laughing, I seem, says he, to be speaking as if I were composing a treatise, but notwithstanding this, it is as I say.

He allowed it.

But I have mentioned these things, in order that you may be of the same opinion as myself. For to me it appears, not only that Magnitude is never willing to be at the same time both great and small, but that the magnitude which we contain never desires to receive that which is small, nor be surpassed; but that it is willing to do one of these two things, either to fly away and gradually withdraw itself, when its contrary the small approaches to it, or to perish when it arrives; but that it is unwilling, by sustaining and receiving Parvitude, to be different from what it was. In the same manner as I myself receiving and sustaining Parvitude, and still remaining that what I am, am small. But that which is great dares not to be small. And in like manner *the small*, which resides in us, is not willing at any time *to subsist in becoming* great, or *to be* great: nor does anything else among contraries, while it remains that which it was, wish at the same time *to subsist in becoming*, and being, its contrary; but it either departs or perishes in consequence of this affection.

It appears so to me, says Cebes, in every respect.

But a certain person, who was present, upon hearing this (I do not clearly remember who it was), By the gods, says he, was not the very contrary of what you now assert admitted by you in the former part of your discourse—viz., that the greater was generated from the less, and the less from the greater; and that generation among contraries plainly took place from contraries? But now you appear to me to say, that this can never be the case. Upon this Socrates, after he had inclined his head, and had listened to his discourse, said, You very manfully put me in mind; yet you do not understand the difference between what is now and what was then asserted. For then it was said, that a contrary thing was generated from a contrary; but now, that the contrary in itself can never become contrary to itself, neither in us, nor in nature. For then, my friend, we spoke concerning things which possess contraries, calling the contraries by the appellation of the things in which they reside; but now we speak of things which receive their denomination from the contraries residing in them. And we should never be willing to assert that these contraries receive a generation from one another. And at the same time, beholding Cebes, he said, Did anything which has been said by this interrogator disturb you also?

Indeed, says Cebes, it did not; and I cannot say that I am not easily disturbed.

We ingenuously, therefore, says he, assent to this, that the contrary can never become contrary to itself.

Entirely so, says Cebes.

But still further, says he, consider whether you agree with me in this also. Do you call *the hot* and *the cold* anything?

I do.

Are they the same with snow and fire?

They are not, by Zeus.

The hot, therefore, is something different from *fire*, and *the cold* from *snow*.

Certainly.

But this also is, I think, apparent to you, that snow, as long as it is such, can never, by receiving heat, remain what it was before—viz., snow, and at the same time become hot; but on the accession of heat, must either withdraw from it, or perish.

Entirely so.

And again, that fire, when cold approaches to it, must either depart or perish; but that it will never dare, by receiving coldness, still to remain what it was—*i.e*, fire, and yet be at the same time cold.

You speak truly, says he.

But, says Socrates, it happens to some of these, that not only the species itself is always thought worthy of the same appellation, but likewise something else, which is not indeed that species, but which perpetually possesses the form of it as long as it exists. But in the following instances my meaning will perhaps be more apparent. The odd number ought always to possess that name by which we now call it: should it not?

Entirely so.

But is this the case with the odd number alone (for this is what I inquire)? or is there anything else which is not indeed the same with the odd, but yet which ought always to be called odd, together with its own proper name, because it naturally subsists in such a manner, that it can never desert the form of the odd? But this is no other than what happens to the number three and many other things. For consider, does not the number three appear to you to be always called by its proper name, and at the same time by the name of the odd, though *the odd* is not the same as *the triad?* Yet the triad, and the pentad, and the entire half of number, naturally subsist in such a manner, that though they are not the same as *the odd*, yet each of them is always odd. And again, two and four, and the whole other order of number, though they are not the same as *the even*, yet each of them is always even: do you admit this or not?

How should I not? says he.

See then, says Socrates, what I wish to evince. But it is as follows: It has appeared, not only that contraries do not receive one another, but that even such things as are not contrary to each other, and yet always possess contraries, do not appear to receive that idea which is contrary to the idea which they contain; but that on its approach they either perish or depart. Shall we not, therefore, say that these things would first perish, and endure anything whatever, sooner than sustain to be three things, and at the same time to be even?

Entirely so, says Cebes.

And yet, says Socrates, the duad is not contrary to the triad.

Certainly not.

Not only therefore, do contrary species never sustain the approach of each other, but certain other things likewise cannot sustain the accession of contraries.

You speak most true, says he.

Are you willing, therefore, says he, that, if we are able, we should define what kind of things these are?

Entirely so.

Will they not, then, Cebes, says he, be such things as compel whatever they occupy, not only to retain their idea, but likewise that of some contrary?

How do you mean?

Exactly as we just now said. For you know it is necessary, that whatever things the idea of three occupies should not only be three, but likewise odd.

Entirely so.

To a thing of this kind, therefore, we assert that an idea contrary to that form, through which it becomes what it is, will never approach.

It cannot.

But it becomes what it is through the odd: does it not?

Certainly.

But is not the contrary to this the idea of the even?

It is.

The idea of the even, therefore, will never accede to three things.

Never.

Are not three things, therefore, destitute of the even?

Destitute.

The triad, therefore, is an odd number.

It is.

The things which I mentioned then are defined—viz., such things, which, though they are not contrary to some particular nature, yet do not at the same time receive it; just as the triad in the present instance, though it is not contrary to the even, yet does not anything more receive it on this account: for it always brings with it that which is contrary to the even; and in like manner the duad to the odd, and fire to cold, and an abundant multitude of other particulars. But see whether you would thus define, not only that a contrary does not receive a contrary, but likewise that the nature which brings with it a contrary to that to which it approaches, will never receive the contrariety of that which it introduces. But recollect again, for it will not be useless to hear it repeated often. Five things will not receive the form of the even; neither will ten things, which are the double of five, receive the form of the odd. This, therefore, though it is itself contrary to something else, yet will not receive the form of the odd; nor will the sesquialter, nor other things of this kind, such as the half and the third part, ever receive the form of the whole, if you pursue and assent to these consequences.

I most vehemently, says he, pursue and assent to them.

Again, therefore, says Socrates, speak to me from the beginning; and this not by answering to what I inquire, but, in a different manner, imitating me. For I say this, in consequence of perceiving another mode of answering, arising from what has now been said, no less secure than that which was established at first. For, if you should ask me what that is, which, when inherent in any body, causes the body to be hot, I should not give you that safe and unskilful answer, that it is heat, but one more elegant deduced from what we have just now said; I mean, that it is fire. Nor, if you should ask me what that is, which when inherent in a certain body, the body is diseased, I should not say that it is disease, but a fever. Nor, if you should ask what that is, which when inherent in a number, the number will be odd, I should not say that it is oddness, but unity, and in a similar manner in other particulars. But see whether you sufficiently understand my meaning.

Perfectly so, says he.

Answer me then, says Socrates, what that is which, when inherent in the body, the body will be alive?

Soul, says he.

Is this then always the case?

How should it not, says he?

Will soul, therefore, always introduce life to that which it occupies?

It will truly, says he.

But is there anything contrary to life, or not?

There is.

But what?

Death.

The soul, therefore, will never receive the contrary to that which it introduces, in consequence of what has been already admitted?

Assuredly it cannot, says Cebes.

But what? how do we denominate that which does not receive the idea of the even?

Odd, says he.

And how do we call that which does not receive justice, and that which does not receive music?

We call, says he, the one unjust, and the other unmusical.

Be it so. But what do we call that which does not receive death?

Immortal, says he.

The soul does not receive death?

It does not.

The soul, therefore, is immortal.

Immortal.

Let it be so, says he. And shall we say that this is now demonstrated? Or how does it appear to you?

It appears to me, Socrates, to be most sufficiently demonstrated.

What then, says he, Cebes, if it were essential to *the odd* that it should be free from destruction, would not three things be indestructible?

How should they not?

If, therefore, it was also essential that a thing void of heat should be indestructible, when any one should introduce heat to snow, would not the snow withdraw itself, safe and unliquefied? For it would not perish; not yet, abiding, would it receive the heat.

You speak the truth, says he.

In like manner, I think if that which is void of cold was indestructible, that when anything cold approached to fire, the fire would neither be extinguished nor destroyed, but would depart free from damage.

It is necessary, says he.

Hence, says Socrates, it is necessary to speak in this manner concerning that which is immortal: for, if that which is immortal is indestructible, it is impossible that the soul, when death approaches to it, should perish. For it follows, from what has been said, that it does not receive death, and of course it will never be dead. Just as we said, that three things will never be even, nor will this ever be the case with that which is odd: nor will fire ever be cold, nor yet the heat which is inherent in fire. But some one may say, What hinders but that the odd may never become the even, through the accession of the even, as we have confessed; and yet, when the odd is destroyed, the even may succeed instead of it? We cannot contend with him who makes this objection, that it is not destroyed: for the odd is not free from destruction; since, if this was granted to us, we might easily oppose the objection, and obtain this concession, that the odd and three things would depart, on the approach of the even; and we might contend in the same manner about fire and heat, and other particulars: might we not?

Entirely so.

And now, therefore, since we have confessed respecting that which is immortal, that it is indestructible, it must follow that the soul is, together with being immortal, likewise indestructible: but if this be not admitted, other arguments will be necessary for our conviction. But there is no occasion for this, says he. For it is scarcely possible that anything else should be void of corruption, if that which is immortal and eternal is subject to dissolution.[1]

But I think, says Socrates, that Divinity, and the form itself of life, and if anything else besides this is immortal, must be confessed by all beings to be entirely free from dissolution. All men, indeed, says he, by Zeus, must acknowledge this; and much more, as it appears to me, must it be admitted by the gods. Since, therefore, that which is immortal is also incorruptible, will not the soul, since it is immortal, be indestructible?

It is perfectly necessary.

When, therefore, death invades a man, the mortal part of him, as it appears, dies; but the immortal part departs safe and uncorrupted, and withdraws itself from death.

It appears so.

The soul, therefore, says he, O Cebes, will, more than

---

[1] Immortality belongs only to the soul. Indestructibility belongs to both body and soul.

anything, be immortal and indestructible ; and our souls will in reality subsist in Hades.

And therefore, says he, Socrates, I have nothing further to object to these arguments, nor any reason why I should disbelieve their reality : but if either Simmias, or any person present, has anything to say, he will do well not to be silent : for I know not what other opportunity he can have, besides the present, if he wishes either to speak or hear about things of this kind.

But indeed, says Simmias, I have nothing which can hinder my belief in what has been said. But yet on account of the magnitude of the things about which we have discoursed, and through my despising human imbecility, I am compelled to retain with myself an unbelief about what has been asserted.

Indeed, Simmias, says Socrates, you not only speak well in the present instance, but it is necessary that even those first hypotheses which we established, and which are believed by us, should at the same time be more clearly considered: and if you sufficiently investigate them, you will follow reason, as it appears to me, in as great a degree as is possible to a man. And if this becomes manifest, you will no longer make any further inquiry.

You speak true, says he.

But it is just, my friends, says he, to think that if the soul is immortal, it requires our care and attention, not only for the present time, in which we say it lives, but likewise with a view to the whole of time : and it will now appear that he who neglects it must subject himself to a most dreadful danger. For, if death were the liberation of the whole man, it would be an unexpected gain to the wicked to be liberated at the same time from the body, and from their vices together with their soul: but now, since the soul appears to be immortal, no other flight from evils, and no other safety remains for it, than in becoming as good and as wise as possible. For when the soul arrives at Hades, it will possess nothing but discipline and education, which are said to be of the greatest advantage or detriment to the dead, in the very beginning of their progression thither. For thus it is said: that the dæmon of each person, which was allotted to him while living, endeavors to lead each to a certain place, where it is necessary that all of them, being collected together, after they have been judged, should proceed to Hades, together with their leader, who is ordered to conduct them from hence thither. But there receiving the allotments proper to their condition, and abiding for a necessary time, another leader brings them back hither again, in many and long periods of time. The journey, therefore, is not such as Telephus asserts it to be in Eschylus. For he says that a single and simple path leads to Hades: but it appears to me that the path is neither simple nor one. For there would be no occasion of leaders, nor could any one ever wander from the right road, if there was but one way. But now it appears to have many divisions and dubious turnings: and this I conjecture from our holy and legal rites. The soul, therefore, which is properly adorned with virtue, and which possesses wisdom, willingly follows its leader, and is not ignorant of its present condition: but the soul which still adheres to body through desire (as I said before), being for a long space of time terrified about it, and struggling and suffering abundantly about the visible place,[1] is with violence and

---

[1] Its place of interment.

great difficulty led away by its presiding dæmon. And when it arrives at that place where other souls are assembled, all the rest fly from and avoid this unpurified soul, which has been guilty of either unjust slaughter, or has perpetrated such deeds as are allied to this, and are the works of kindred souls; nor is any one willing to become either its companion or leader. But such a soul wanders about, oppressed with every kind of anxiety and trouble, till certain periods of time are accomplished: and these being completed, it is driven by necessity to an abode accommodated to its nature. But the soul which has passed through life with purity and moderation, obtaining the gods for its companions and leaders, will reside in a place adapted to its purified condition.

There are indeed many and admirable places belonging to the earth; and the earth itself is neither of such a kind, nor of such a magnitude, as those who are accustomed to speak about it imagine, as I am persuaded from a certain person's account.

How is this, Socrates, says Simmias? For I myself also have heard many things about the earth; and yet perhaps not these particulars which have obtained your belief. I should therefore be glad to hear you relate them.

Indeed, Simmias, says he, the art of Glaucus does not appear to me to be necessary,[1] in order to relate these particulars; but to evince their truth, seems to me to be an undertaking beyond what the art of Glaucus can accomplish. Besides, I myself perhaps am not able to accomplish this; and even though I should know how, the time which is allotted me to live, Simmias, seems by

---

[1] A proverb of unknown origin, about matters requiring little trouble.

no means sufficient for the length of such a discourse. However, nothing hinders me from informing you what I am persuaded is the truth, respecting the form of the earth, and the places which it contains.

And this information, says Simmias, will be sufficient.

I am persuaded, therefore, says he, in the first place, that if the earth is in the middle of the heavens, and is of a spherical figure, it has no occasion of air, nor of any other such like necessity, to prevent it from falling: but that the perfect similitude of the heavens to themselves, and the equilibrity of the earth, are sufficient causes of its support. For that which is equally inclined, when placed in the middle of a similar nature, cannot tend more or less to one part than another; but, subsisting on all sides similarly affected, it will remain free from all inclination. This is the first thing of which I am persuaded.

And very properly so, says Cebes.

But yet further, says he, that the earth is prodigiously great; that we who dwell in places extending from Phasis to the pillars of Hercules, inhabit only a small portion of it, about the Mediterranean Sea, like ants or frogs about a marsh; and that there are many others elsewhere, who dwell in many such-like places. For I am persuaded, that there are everywhere about the earth many hollow places of all-various forms and magnitudes; into which there is a confluence of water, mists and air: but that the earth itself, which is of a pure nature, is situated in the pure heavens, in which the stars are contained, and which most of those who are accustomed to speak about such particulars denominate æther. But the places which we inhabit are nothing more than the dregs of this pure earth, or cavities into which its dregs continually flow. We are ignorant, therefore, that we dwell in the cavities of this earth, and imagine that we inhabit its upper parts. Just as if some one dwelling in the middle bottom of the sea, should think that he resided on its surface, and, beholding the sun and other stars through the water, should imagine that the sea is the heavens: but through sloth and imbecility having never ascended to the top of the sea, nor emerged from its deeps into this region, has never perceived how much purer and more beautiful it is than the place which he inhabits, nor has received this information from any other who has beheld this place of our abode. In the very same manner are we affected: for, dwelling in a certain hollow of the earth, we think that we reside on its surface; and we call the air heaven, as if the stars passed through this, as through the heavens themselves. And this likewise, in the same manner as in the above instance, happens to us through our imbecility and sloth, which render us incapable of ascending to the summit of the air. For, otherwise, if any one could arrive at its summit, or, becoming winged, could fly thither, he would be seen emerging from hence; and just as fishes, emerging hither from the sea, perceive what our region contains, in the same manner would he behold the several particulars belonging to the summit of the earth. And besides this, if his nature was sufficient for such an elevated survey, he would know that the heavens which he there beheld were the true heavens, and that he perceived the true light and the true earth. For this earth which we inhabit, the stones which it contains, and the whole region of our abode, are all corrupted and gnawed, just as things in the sea are corroded by the salt: for nothing worthy of estimation grows in the sea, nor does it contain anything perfect; but caverns and sand, and immense quantities of mud and filth, are found in it wherever there is earth. Nor are its contents to be by any means compared with the beauty of the various particulars in our place of abode. But those upper regions of the earth will appear to be yet far more excellent than these which we inhabit. For, if it is proper to tell you a beautiful fable, it is well worth hearing, Simmias, what kind of places those are on the upper earth, situated under the heavens.

And gladly should we hear it, O Socrates, said Simmias.

It is reported then, my friend, says he, in the first place, that this earth, if any one surveys it from on high, appears like those balls which are covered with twelve pieces of leather, various, and distinguished with colors; a pattern of which are the colors found among us, and which our painters use. But there the whole earth is composed from materials of this kind, and such as are much more splendid and pure than our region contains: for they are partly indeed purple, and endued with a wonderful beauty; partly of a golden color; and partly more white than plaster or snow; and are composed from other colors in a similar manner, and those more in number and more beautiful than we have ever beheld. For the hollow parts of this pure earth, being filled with water and air, exhibit a certain species of color, shining among the variety of other colors in such a manner, that from any one view the earth is always varicolored. Hence, whatever grows in this earth grows analogous to its nature, such as its trees, and flowers, and fruits: and again, its mountains and stones possess a similar perfection and transparency, and are rendered beautiful through various colors; of which the stones so much honored by us in this place of our abode are but small parts, such as sardin-stones, jaspers and emeralds, and all of this kind. But there nothing subsists which is not of such a nature as I have described; and there are other things far more beautiful than even these. But the reason of this is because the stones there are pure, and not consumed and corrupted, like ours, through rottenness and salt, from a conflux of various particulars, which in our places of abode cause filthiness and disease to the stones and earth, animals and plants, which are found among us. But this pure earth is adorned with all these, and with gold and silver, and other things of a similar nature: for all these are naturally apparent, since they are both numerous and large, and are diffused everywhere throughout the earth; so that to behold it is the spectacle of blessed spectators. This earth too contains many other animals and men, some of whom inhabit its middle parts; others dwell about the air, as we do about the sea; and others reside in islands which the air flows round, and which are situated not far from the continent. And in one word, what water and the sea are to us, with respect to utility, that air is to them: but what air is to us, that æther is to the inhabitants of this pure earth. But the seasons there are endued with such an excellent temperament, that the inhabitants are never molested with disease, and live for a much longer time than those who dwell in our regions; and they surpass us in sight, hearing and wisdom, and everything of this kind, as much as air excels water in purity—and æther, air. And besides this, they have groves and temples of the gods, in which the gods dwell in reality; and likewise oracles and divinations, and sensible perceptions of the gods, and such-like associations with them. The sun too, and moon and stars, are seen by them such as they really are; and in every other respect their felicity is of a correspondent nature.

And in this manner indeed the whole earth naturally subsists, and the parts which are situated about it. But it contains about the whole of its ambit many places in its concavities; some of which are more profound and extended than the region which we inhabit: but others are more profound, indeed, but yet have a less chasm than the places of our abode; and there are certain parts which are less profound, but broader than ours. But all these are in many places perforated into one another under the earth, according to narrower and broader avenues, and have passages of communication through which a great quantity of water flows into the different hollows of the earth, as into bowls; and besides this, there are immense bulks of ever-flowing rivers under the earth, and of hot and cold waters; likewise a great quantity of fire, mighty rivers of fire, and many of moist mire, some of which are purer, and others more muddy; as in Sicily there are rivers of mud, which flow before a stream of fire, which is itself a flaming torrent. And from these the several places are filled, into which each flows at particular times. But all these are moved upwards and downwards, like a swinging or oscillation in the earth. And this is the cause of it: There is a chasm in the earth, and this the greatest, and totally perforated through the whole earth. And of this Homer thus speaks—

> Far, very far, where under earth is found
> A gulf, of every depth, the most profound:[1]

[1] Iliad; book viii, verse 14.

which he elsewhere and many other poets denominate Tartarus. For into this chasm there is a conflux of all rivers, from which they again flow upwards. But each derives its quality from the earth through which it flows. And the reason why they all flow into, and again out of this chasm, is because this moisture cannot find either a bottom or a basis. Hence it swings and seethes upwards and downwards: and this, too, is the case with the air and wind which are situated about it. For they follow this moisture, both when they are impelled to more remote places of the earth, and when to the places of our abode. And as in respiration the flowing breath is perpetually expired and inspired, so there the wind, which is swayed about together with the moisture, causes certain vehement and immense winds during its ingress and departure. When the water, therefore, being impelled, flows into that place which we call downwards, then the river flows through the earth into different channels, and fills them; just as those who pour into another vessel the water which they have drawn. But when this water, departing from thence, is impelled hither, it again fills the rivers on the earth; and these, when filled, flow through channels and through the earth; and when they have severally passed through the avenues, which are open to each, they produce seas, lakes, rivers and fountains. Flowing back again from hence under the earth, and some of them streaming round longer and more numerous places, but others round such as are shorter and less numerous, they again hurl themselves into Tartarus; and some indeed much more profoundly, but others less so, than they were drawn; but the influxions of all of them are deeper than the places from which they flow upwards. And the effluxions of some are on a side opposite to their influxions, but in others both take place on the same side. There are some again which entirely flow round in a circle, folding themselves like snakes, once or often about the earth; and tending downwards as much as possible, they again fall into the chasm. On every side the rivers can descend to the center, but not beyond it, for the part opposite to both directions is steep.

The other rivers, indeed, are many, great and various: but among this abundance there are certain streams, four in number, of which the greatest, and which circularly flows round the earth the outermost of all, is called the Ocean. But that which flows opposite, and in a contrary direction to this, is Acheron; which, flowing through other solitary places, and under the earth, devolves its waters into the Acherusian marsh, into which many souls of the dead pass; and abiding there for certain destined spaces of time, some of which are more and others less extended, they are again sent into the generations of animals. The third river of these hurls itself forth in the middle, and near its source falls into a mighty place, burning with abundance of fire, and produces a lake greater than our sea, and hot with water and mud. But it proceeds from hence, turbulent and miry, and, encircling the earth, arrives both elsewhere and at the extremities of the Acherusian marsh, with the water of which it does not become mingled; but often revolving itself under the earth, flows into the more downward parts of Tartarus. And this is the river which they still denominate Pyriphlegethon; the streams of which burst up in gushes in various parts of the earth. But the fourth river, which is opposite to this, first falls as it is said into a place dreadful and wild, and wholly tinged with a gloomy color, which they denominate Styx: and the influxive streams of this river form the Stygian marsh. But falling into this, and receiving vehement powers in its waters, it hides itself under the earth, and rolling round, proceeds contrary to Pyriphlegethon, and meets with it in the Acherusian marsh in a contrary direction. Nor is the water of this river mingled with anything, but, revolving in a circle, it hurls itself into Tartarus in a course opposite to Pyriphlegethon. But its name, according to the poets, is Cocytus.

These being thus naturally constituted, when the dead arrive at that place into which the dæmon leads each, in the first place they are judged, as well those who have lived in a becoming manner, and piously and justly, as those who have not. And those who appear to have passed a middle kind of life, proceeding to Acheron, and ascending the vehicles prepared for them, arrive in these at the Acherusian lake, and dwell there; till being purified, and having suffered punishment for any injuries they may have committed, they are enlarged; and each receives the reward of his beneficence according to his deserts. But those who appear to be incurable, through the magnitude of their offenses, because they have perpetrated either many and great sacrileges, or many unjust slaughters, and such as are contrary to law, or other things of this kind—these, a destiny adapted to their guilt hurls into Tartarus, from which they will never be discharged. But those who are found to have committed curable, but yet mighty crimes, such as those who have been guilty through anger of any violence against their father or mother, and have lived the remainder of their lives penitent for the offense, or who have become homicides in any other similar manner; with respect to these, it is necessary that they should fall into Tartarus: but after they have fallen, and have dwelt there for a year, the waves hurl them out of Tartarus; and the ordinary homicides indeed into Cocytus, but the slayers of fathers and mothers into Pyriphlegethon. But when, being borne along by these rivers, they arrive at the Acherusian marsh, they here bellow and invoke those whom they have slaughtered or injured. But, invoking these, they suppliantly entreat that they would suffer them to enter into the lake, and forgive them. And if they persuade them to do this, they depart, and find an end to their maladies: but if they are unable to accomplish this, they are carried back again into Tartarus, and from thence again into the rivers. And they do not cease from suffering this, till they have persuaded those they have injured to forgiveness. For this punishment was ordained them by the judges. But those who shall appear to have lived most excellently, with respect to piety—these are they, who, being liberated and dismissed from these places in the earth, as from the abodes of a prison, shall arrive at the pure habitation on high, and dwell on the ætherial earth. And among these, those who are sufficiently purified by philosophy shall live without bodies, through the whole of the succeeding time, and shall arrive at habitations yet more beautiful than these, which is neither easy to describe, nor is the present time sufficient for such an undertaking.

But for the sake of these particulars which we have related, we should undertake everything, Simmias, that we may participate of virtue and prudence in the present life. For the reward is beautiful, and the hope mighty.

To affirm, indeed, that these things subsist exactly as I have described them, is not the province of a man endued with intellect. But to assert that either these or certain particulars of this kind take place, with respect to our souls and their habitations—since our soul appears to be immortal—this is, I think, both becoming, and deserves to be hazarded by him who believes in its reality. For the risk is a noble one, and we must allure ourselves with things of this kind, as with enchantments: and on this account, I produced the fable which you have just now heard me relate. But, for the sake of these, it is proper that the man should be confident about his soul, who in the present life bidding farewell to those pleasures which regard the body and its ornaments, as things foreign from its nature, has earnestly applied himself to disciplines, as things of far greater consequence; and who having adorned his soul not with a foreign but its own proper ornament—viz., with temperance and justice, fortitude, liberty and truth, expects a migration to Hades, as one who is ready to depart whenever he shall be called upon by Fate. You, therefore, says he, Simmias and Cebes, and the rest who are here assembled, will each depart in some period of time posterior to the present; but

Me now calling, Fate demands:

(as some tragic poet would say) and it is almost time that I should betake myself to the bath. For it appears to me better to wash myself before I drink the poison, and not to trouble the women with washing my dead body.

When, therefore, he had thus spoken,—Be it so, Socrates, says Crito: but what orders do you leave to these who are present, or to myself, or respecting your children, or anything else in the execution of which we can particularly oblige you?

None such as are new, says he, Crito, but that which I have always said to you; that if you take care of yourselves, you will always perform in whatever you do that which is acceptable to myself, to my family, and to your own selves, though you should not promise me anything at present. But if you neglect yourselves, and are unwilling to live according to what has been now and formerly said, as vestiges of direction in your course, you will accomplish nothing, though you should now promise many things, and in a very vehement manner.

We shall take care, therefore, says Crito, to act as you desire. But how would you be buried?

Just as you please, says he, if you can but catch me, and I do not escape from you. And at the same time gently laughing, and addressing himself to us, I cannot persuade Crito, says he, my friends, that I am that Socrates who now disputes with you, and orders every part of the discourse; but he thinks that I am he whom he will shortly behold dead, and asks how I ought to be buried. But all that long discourse which some time since I addressed to you, in which I asserted that after I had drunk the poison I should no longer remain with you, but should depart to certain felicities of the blessed, this I seem to have declared to him in vain, though it was undertaken to console both you and myself. Promise, therefore, says he, for me to Crito, just the contrary of what he promised to my judges. For he promised that I should not run away; but do you engage that when I die I shall not stay with you, but shall depart and entirely leave you; that Crito may more easily bear this separation, and may not be afflicted when he sees my body either burnt or buried, as if I suffered some dreadful misfortune; and that he may not say at my interment, that Socrates is laid out, or is carried out, or is buried. For be well assured of this, says he, excellent Crito, that when we do not speak in a becoming manner, we are not only culpable with respect to our speech, but likewise affect our souls with a certain evil. But it is proper to be confident, and to say that my body will be buried, and in such a manner as is pleasing to you, and which you think is most agreeable to our laws.

When he had thus spoken he rose, and went into a certain room, that he might wash himself, and Crito followed him: but he ordered us to wait for him. We waited, therefore, accordingly, discoursing over and reviewing among ourselves what had been said; and sometimes speaking about his death, how great a calamity it would be to us; and sincerely thinking that we, like those who are deprived of their father, should pass the rest of our life in the condition of orphans. But when he had washed himself, his sons were brought to him (for he had two little ones, and one considerably advanced in age), and the women belonging to his family likewise came in to him: but when he had spoken to them before Crito, and had left them such injunctions as he thought proper, he ordered the boys and women to depart; and he himself returned to us. And it was now near the setting of the sun: for he had been absent for a long time in the bathing-room. But when he came in from washing, he sat down; and did not speak much afterwards. For then the servant of the eleven magistrates came in, and standing near him, I do not perceive that in you, Socrates, says he, which I have taken notice of in others; I mean, that they are angry with me, and curse me, when, being compelled by the magistrates, I announce to them that they must drink the poison. But, on the contrary, I have found you at the present time to be the most generous, mild and the best of all the men that ever came into this place: and, therefore, I am well convinced that you are not angry with me, but with the authors of your present condition. You know those whom I allude to. Now, therefore (for you know what I came to tell you), farewell, and endeavor to bear this necessity as easily as possible. And at the same time bursting into tears, and turning himself away, he departed.

But Socrates looking after him, And thou too, says he, farewell; and we shall take care to act as you advise. And at the same time turning to us, How courteous, says he, is the behavior of that man! During the whole time of my abode here, he has visited and often conversed with me, and proved himself to be the best of men; and now how generously he weeps on my account! But let us obey him, Crito, and let some one bring the poison, if it is bruised; but if not, let the man whose business it is bruise it himself.

But, Socrates, says Crito, I think that the sun still hangs over the mountains, and is not yet set. And at the same time I have known others who have drunk the poison very late, after it was announced to them; who have supped and drunk abundantly; and who have enjoyed converse with whomsoever they desire. Therefore, do not be in such haste; for there is yet time enough.

Upon this Socrates replied, Such men, Crito, act with great propriety in the manner you have described (for they think to derive some advantage by so doing), and I also with great propriety shall not act in this manner. For I do not think I shall gain anything by drinking it later, except becoming ridiculous to myself through desiring to live, and being sparing of life when nothing of it any longer remains. Go, then, says he, be persuaded, and comply with my request.

Then Crito, hearing this, gave the sign to the boy that stood near him. And the boy departing and having stayed for some time, came, bringing with him the person that was to administer the poison, and who brought it properly prepared in a cup. But Socrates, beholding the man—It is well, my friend, says he; but what is proper to do with it? for you are knowing in these affairs.

You have nothing else to do, says he, but when you have drunk it to walk about, till a heaviness takes place in your legs; and afterwards lie down: this is the manner in which you should act. And at the same time he extended the cup to Socrates. But Socrates received it from him—and indeed, Echecrates, with great cheerfulness; neither trembling, nor suffering any alteration for the worse in his color or countenance: but, as he was accustomed to do, beholding the man with a bull-like aspect, What say you, says he, respecting this potion? Is it lawful to make a libation of it, or not?

We only bruise, says he, Socrates, as much as we think sufficient for the purpose.

I understand you, says he: but it is certainly both lawful and proper to pray to the gods, that my departure from hence thither may be attended with prosperous fortune; which I entreat them to grant may be the case. And at the same time ending his discourse, he drank the poison with exceeding facility and alacrity. And thus far, indeed, the greater part of us were tolerably well able to refrain from weeping; but when we saw him drinking, and that he had drunk it, we could no longer restrain our tears. But from me, indeed, notwithstanding the violence which I employed in checking them, they flowed abundantly; so that, covering myself with my mantle, I deplored my misfortune. I did not indeed weep for him, but for my own fortune; considering what an associate I should be deprived of. But Crito, who was not able to restrain his tears, was compelled to rise before me. And Apollodorus, who during the whole time prior to this had not ceased from weeping, then wept aloud with great bitterness; so that he infected all who were present, except Socrates. But Socrates, upon seeing this, exclaimed— What are you doing, excellent men? For, indeed, I principally sent away the women, lest they should produce a disturbance of this kind. For I have heard that it is proper to die joyfully and with propitious omens. Be quiet, therefore, and summon fortitude to your assistance.

When we heard this we blushed, and restrained our tears. But he, when he found during his walking that his legs felt heavy, and had told us so, laid himself down in a supine position. For the man had ordered him to do so. And at the same time he who gave him the poison, touching him at intervals, considered his feet and legs. And after he had vehemently pressed his foot, he asked him if he felt it. But Socrates answered he did not. And after this he again pressed his thighs: and thus ascending with his hand, he showed us that he was cold and stiff. And Socrates also touched himself, and said, that when the poison reached his heart he should then leave us.

But now his lower belly was almost cold; when uncovering his face (for he was covered), he said (which were his last words):

Crito, we owe a cock to Asclepius.[1] Discharge this debt, therefore for me, and do not neglect it.

It shall be done, says Crito: but consider whether you have any other commands. To this inquiry of Crito he made no reply; but shortly after moved himself, and the man uncovered him. And his eyes were fixed; which when Crito perceived, he closed his mouth and eyes. This, Echecrates, was the end of our associate; a man, as it appears to me, the best of the men of that time with whom we were acquainted, and besides this, the most wise and just.

---

[1] The sacrifice paid on recovery from an illness.

www.ingramcontent.com/pod-product-compliance
Lightning Source LLC
Chambersburg PA
CBHW030333170426
43202CB00010B/1114